PRINCE® 2

PRINCE® 2
A PRACTICAL HANDBOOK

COLIN BENTLEY

BUTTERWORTH
HEINEMANN

Butterworth-Heinemann
Linacre House, Jordan Hill, Oxford OX2 8DP
225 Wildwood Avenue, Woburn, MA 01801-2041
A division of Reed Educational and Professional Publishing Ltd

A member of the Reed Elsevier plc group

OXFORD   AUCKLAND   BOSTON
JOHANNESBURG   MELBOURNE   NEW DELHI

First published 1997
Reprinted 1998, 1999

British Library Cataloguing in Publication Data
A catalogue record for this book is available from the Library of Congress

ISBN 0 7506 3240 2

Printed and bound in Great Britain by
Biddles Ltd, Guildford and King's Lynn

FOR EVERY TITLE THAT WE PUBLISH, BUTTERWORTH-HEINEMANN
WILL PAY FOR BTCV TO PLANT AND CARE FOR A TREE.

Contents

1 | Introduction

What is a Project?

A project can be defined as having:

- The solution of a business need as its driving force
- A defined and unique set of products
- A corresponding set of activities to construct the products
- Appropriate resources to undertake the activities
- A finite life-span
- An organisational structure with defined responsibilities.

The Need for a Project Management Method

There are four major aims for any project:

- To deliver the required end-product(s)
- To meet the specified quality
- To stay within budget
- To deliver on schedule.

There are many examples of projects which fail to meet one or more of these aims. Many projects have weak areas which may contribute to failure to meet the aims. Examples which might ring a bell with the reader are:

- Failure to involve the customer throughout the project
- Lack of communication across the team and between management and those developing the solution
- Confusion about what is required

- Lack of understanding caused by the use of jargon
- Personnel changes in the management of a project which cause confusion by introducing a totally different style of management
- Products not checked or inadequately checked for quality.

If an organisation has a project management method, it stands a better chance of achieving successful projects. If all projects in the organisation use the same method, there will be more consistency in the approach to projects and reporting progress, transfer of management staff across projects will be less of a problem.

If the method used is a proven one, it will address the above aims and areas of weakness and contain components which, applied correctly, will avoid the pitfalls and act as a guide to successful projects.

The successful use of a project management method needs training and commitment. Not only the commitment of the project managers, but more importantly the commitment of senior management. There is no point in senior management saying 'Get on with the job', then distancing themselves from the decision-making needed during the project, but being ready to blame the project manager for any failure at the end.

What is PRINCE 2?

PRINCE is a development of PROMPT II, the proprietary project management methodology which was adopted by the CCTA in 1979 as the standard for government IT departments. PROMPT II was developed by a company called Simpact Systems, later taken over by Learmonth and Burchett Management Systems. The CCTA added a number of enhancements and changes to the original methodology and put the resulting PRINCE methodology in the public domain in 1989.

PRINCE 2 is a new version of the method introduced on the 1st October 1996. It is now a methodology for management of any type or size of project, not just for computer system development. It is still compatible with the system development methodologies used in government IT projects, and accommodates their use for the technical aspects of development.

From the description of the aims of a project in the previous section it is easy to trace the PRINCE philosophy that project management must be built around:

- The products required by the customer (or user)

- The activities needed to produce those products

- A method of planning which starts from the required products and incorporates the derived activities

- A series of controls also based on those products which cover quality, schedule and cost

- An organisational structure which defines the essential roles, responsibilities, levels of decision-making and lines of communication

- A statement of the project management steps required to start a project, control its evolution and bring it to a conclusion, and those steps interlinked with the other components described above.

PRINCE 2 offers a process-based approach to key areas of project management. It covers:

- The steps in managing a project

- Project organisation

- Planning

- Control.

It interfaces with existing and well-proven techniques and procedures such as:

- People management techniques, such as motivation and team leadership styles

- Network planning

- Bar charting

- The management of risk.

PRINCE 2 Overview

PRINCE 2 consists of a series of processes which contain the steps which need to be considered in the management of a project, components for the organisation, planning and control of a project, supported by a number of techniques – product-based planning, quality review and change control. There are linkages between all these elements and they complement one another in one cohesive method.

THE PRINCE 2 PROCESSES

There are eight processes, shown in Figure 1-1. These cover the different events in the project.

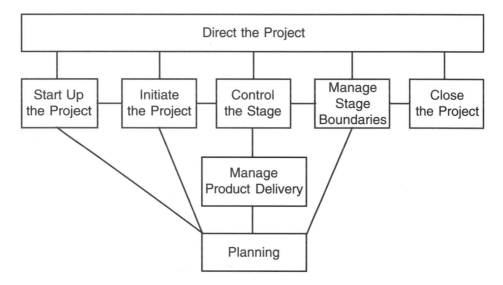

Figure 1-1. The PRINCE 2 Processes

Briefly, the purpose of the processes is:

SU – Start Up the Project	Set up the project management team Establish the terms of reference Decide the way in which a solution will be provided Plan the production of the Project Initiation Document

IP – Initiate the Project	Prepare the Business Case Plan the project Plan the first stage in detail Assess the risks
CS – Control the Stage	Authorise work Check quality Control changes Monitor and control progress
MP – Manage Product Delivery	(This is for the third party team) Agree the work to be done Do the work Report progress to the Project Manager Ensure quality is checked Return the completed work
SB – Manage Stage Boundaries	Plan the next stage Report on the results of the current stage Reassess the Business Case, risks and overall project situation
CP – Close the Project	Hand over the final products Write up any useful lessons Make a list of any follow-on work Plan the assessment of the achievement of the expected benefits
PL – Planning	This is a common process, used by several others which need to create plans
DP – Direct the Project	(This is the senior management (Project Board) process) Authorise initiation of the project (after SU) Authorise the project (after IP) Authorise each stage (after SB) Give advice when sought (during CS) Confirm the project can close (after CP)

PRINCE 2 Components

Organisation

A key concern of PRINCE is that at the outset and throughout the project everyone is clear on who is involved in the project and in what capacity.

The project organisation structure covers the needs of senior management, the customer, the provider of funds, the supplier, the project manager, team managers (if needed), project support (if needed) and an independent assurance capability.

PRINCE defines responsibilities at each level in a series of roles. To cater for different sizes of project, these roles can be combined (for small projects) or shared. The whole project management team is tuned to the specific needs of each project so that it is not over-bureaucratic, but clarifies communication lines, who does what, who is accountable for what and who takes what decisions.

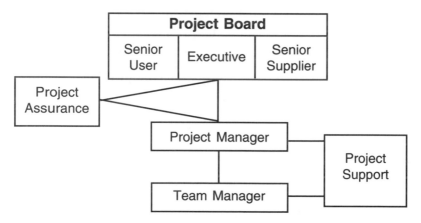

Figure 1-2. The PRINCE 2 Project Organisation Structure

The **Project Board** represents senior management. The **Senior User** role represents the users of the project's end product. The **Executive** represents the customer and the **Senior Supplier** represents the resources which will provide the end product. These roles make the key decisions and commitments of resources. They are usually part-time roles.

The **Project Manager** has day-to-day control of the project and is responsible for planning, monitoring and reporting to the Project Board at identified events and times.

If the project size or complexity warrants it, there may be more than one team contributing towards the end product. If so, there is a **Team Manager** role which describes the responsibilities and the interfaces with the Project Manager.

The Project Manager may need help with such activities as collecting progress information, updating plans, keeping track of change requests, the safekeeping of products which have been developed and other filing. Such optional administrative roles are described under **Project Support.**

The Project Board is accountable for assuring itself that all is well with the project. If the members do not have the requisite skills or the time, they can delegate assurance work to separate **Project Assurance** roles.

Controls

PRINCE provides controls and reports for three levels, the Project Board, the Project Manager and, if used, the Team Manager.

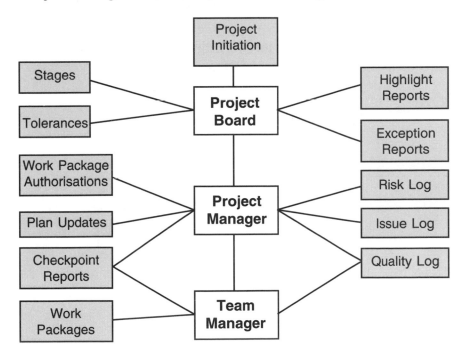

Figure 1-3. An Overview of PRINCE 2 Controls

Initiation of the project is done for the Project Board to decide if the project is viable before spending serious money on it. The project is divided into **Stages**, and the Project Board only commits to one stage at a time. During a stage it receives **Highlight Reports** from the Project Manager. The Project Board sets deviation limits (**Tolerances**) for each stage. Any forecast that these limits are likely to be exceeded means that the Project Manager must advise the Project Board by **Exception Reports** immediately and offer a recommended course of action so that the Project Board can decide what action to take. The Project Board also confirms that objectives have been met and the project is wrapped up with no loose ends before allowing **project closure**.

The Project Manager tracks progress against stage plans and receives **Checkpoint Reports** from the team or teams. Change requests are all recorded and controlled on the **Issue Log**. Risks are continually monitored via the **Risk Log** and quality work observed via the **Quality Log**. Work to be done by teams is controlled by **Work Package Authorisations**.

The Team Manager negotiates **Work Packages** with the Project Manager, maintains the **Quality Log** for work done and reports progress to the Project Manager via **Checkpoint Reports**.

Plans

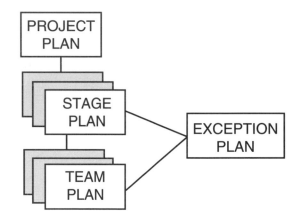

Figure 1-4. PRINCE 2 Plan Overview

The one mandatory plan in PRINCE is the **Project Plan**. This is a high-level plan showing when the key products will be produced and the project cost. It is produced at the outset to prove that the target is achievable and as part of the information on which the Project Board decides if it wishes to proceed with the project. It is updated at the end of each stage and is part of the controls of the Project Board when deciding whether the project should continue into the next stage.

Often the length of the project means that it is not sensible for the Project Manager to put into the Project Plan the level of detail needed to control on a day-to-day basis. A **Stage Plan** can be produced immediately before the stage is to be done. It covers only one stage and the Project Manager can use the information on what has happened in previous stages to reduce the guesswork in the next stage plan.

Where the project is large and has more than one team working on it, there is an option to produce **Team Plans**. This is particularly relevant for teams from third parties, outside contractors.

Where there is a risk of a Stage or Team Plan deviating outside the limits set by the Project Board, the board will most likely ask the Project Manager to produce an **Exception Plan**. This is a re-plan of the remainder of the current plan to reflect the new situation.

The Benefits of using PRINCE 2

- Its use is free
- It is supported by the CCTA and the APM (Association of Project Managers)
- Its owners are working closely with the British Standards Institute to ensure future compatibility with any standards related to project management
- It has a strong user group
- Its owners are committed to a programme of continual improvement
- It has a successful track record stretching back to 1975
- It is fully compatible with the ISEB project management qualification
- It is supported by an increasing number of support tools
- There are many independent companies offering training and consultancy in the method

- A large and increasing number of companies use the method
- Most government departments, their suppliers and the large utility companies already use it

2 | PRINCE 1 and PRINCE 2 Differences

There may be a number of readers who have experience of the first version of PRINCE and who wish to know what changes have been made to the methodology. This chapter lists the changes and describes them, together with the reasoning behind the changes.

Readers who are new to PRINCE may wish to skip this chapter.

The official manual on PRINCE 2 is published by The Stationery Office (previously known as HMSO).

IT REFERENCES REMOVED

All IT references have been removed. The intention is that PRINCE 2 be considered a project management methodology for *any* type of project. In Version 1 there was an overlap between PRINCE and SSADM, the CCTA recommended set of analysis and design techniques for computer projects. All such references have now been removed.

CUSTOMER/SUPPLIER ENVIRONMENT

The methodology is now written from a Customer/supplier viewpoint. This means that the methodology assumes that the customer with the problem and the supplier of the solution may have separate managements. Other scenarios are covered, but the main bulk of the methodology is written from this basis.

SUITABLE FOR SMALL PROJECTS

The methodology also tries to take an approach which will not frighten off small projects. There is much more emphasis on deciding how formal or informal information-passing and decision-making needs to be, based on the individual project's needs. In many cases, the methodology now suggests that information can be exchanged and decisions taken without the need for formal documents and/or meetings.

The Organisation component, for example, puts the assurance responsibilities in the role descriptions for the Project Board members, and suggests that only if the project warrants it should the work of assurance be delegated to others.

PROCESSES

If we think about ISO 9001, we can recognise that it requires each process in the production of a product to be documented. As part of closer alignment with the needs of ISO 9001, therefore, the 'steps' to take in project management within PRINCE are defined in a series of processes. These are:

SU   Start up the Project

New. This covers the pre-project work which was left very vague in PRINCE Version 1. It covers appointment of the Project Board and Project Manager, preparation of the Project Brief and Initiation Stage Plan. A new product is introduced, the Project Mandate. This is a general term, covering the initial request to do the job. The work of the process SU is to turn this into a Project Brief, i.e. something with the information required by PRINCE. (Note: So the **PRINCE** life cycle is now longer than a **project** life cycle.)

IP   Initiate the Project

It is now made clear that initiation starts with a Project Initiation Meeting (PIM), based on the material provided by the process SU. This is the start of the project life cycle.

DP   Direct the Project

This covers the Project Board work, giving it greater emphasis than PRINCE Version 1. It has five sub-processes, 'Authorising Initiation', 'Authorising a Project' (approving the Project Initiation Document), 'Authorising a Stage or Exception Plan', 'Ad Hoc Direction' and 'Authorising Project Closure'.

CS   Control the Stage

This covers the authorisation of work, tracking actuals, capturing and analysing issues, reviewing stage status and escalating exception situations.

MP   Manage Product Delivery

This is to cover the use of sub-contractors. It interfaces with the process CS. The interface is a Work Package which is authorised in process CS. In the process MP details of the Work Package are negotiated with the Project Manager. Other steps in the process handle execution of the work and delivery back to the Project Manager.

SB   Manage Stage Boundaries

This covers ending one stage and starting another. It includes the creation of Exception Plans.

CP   Close the Project

As the title suggests, this interfaces with the appropriate steps of the DP process. The management products have been changed. We now have an End Project Report, a Lessons Learned Report (the old PER) and Follow-on Action Recommendations. The latter wraps up any unclosed Project Issues more neatly than PRINCE Version 1 did.

PL   Planning

This is a common planning process used by several of the other processes.

Each process is broken down into sub-processes.

ORGANISATION

Assurance is now more clearly identified as a Project Board responsibility. The work of assurance can be delegated to assurance people (the old co-ordinators) if, for example, the size or complexity of the project suggest this. This is to avoid small projects feeling that the use of PRINCE would need too much overhead, and reinforces the Project Board's responsibilities as 'owner' of the project. It also emphasises the independence of assurance, describes the potential link with any independent Quality Assurance function and gets away from the PRINCE Version 1 practice, where the Project Assurance Team (PAT) had become part of the Project Manager's team, e.g. the Business Assurance Co-ordinator (BAC) often being involved in the creation and update of plans. This was thought to have destroyed the independence of the assurance function, which is correspondingly upgraded.

The Stage Manager role name has been changed to Team Manager. According to the views of PRINCE Version 1 users, very little use was being made of the Stage Manager role in its pure sense, but very often a Project Manager would find him- or herself controlling work via a number of teams. There was also the need to deal with the environment where the Project Manager was part of the customer's organisation, but much of the work was being done by contractors. It was felt that the name of Team Manager was more flexible and applicable to more project organisation situations.

Project Support has been brought back as administrative support to the Project Manager where needed. This is to absorb those jobs often done by members of the PAT which were felt to affect their independence and, hence, their capability to carry out assurance on behalf of the Project Board.

RISK MANAGEMENT

This gets much more exposure (forgive the pun) in PRINCE 2. There is now a Risk Log, a component chapter on Risk in the official manual and the processes also stress the need to review all risks throughout the project. The methodology stresses that its approach to risk is compatible with the CCTA publication on Management of Risk.

PROJECT EXCEPTIONS

There is now more emphasis on the Project Manager *forecasting* a deviation beyond tolerances, rather than reacting to a deviation which has already happened. The interface is an Exception Report which contains the text of :

- Problem
- Options
- Impact on Business Case and risks
- Recommendation.

The Project Board response will normally cause the Project Manager to raise an Exception Plan. This now has a format like any other PRINCE plan. An Exception Plan is presented at a Mid Stage Assessment. All of the other purposes for a Mid Stage Assessment in PRINCE Version 1 have been dropped, i.e. you don't have a Mid Stage Assessment in the middle of a long stage, you break the stage into two or more stages.

TECHNICAL

The term is dropped, mainly because there was a tie in to IT terminology with the constant use of 'technical'. 'Senior Technical' becomes 'Senior Supplier', 'Technical Exceptions' are now 'Project Issues'. The separation of Technical and Resource plans is no longer made. As most people use a piece of software as a planning tool which can generate both types of report from the one plan, the old distinction is felt to be unnecessary.

QUALITY

The Quality Review is still there, but it is pointed out that it is only one type of quality check. A Quality Log is introduced to keep a record of **all** quality checks done.

ISO 9001

There is a much closer relationship between PRINCE 2 and ISO 9001. PRINCE 2 still does not meet all the requirements of the quality standard, because a number of the ISO standards apply to an entire site or company, rather than an individual project. An Appendix to the official PRINCE 2 manual describes the sections of ISO 9001 and relates PRINCE 2 to each one.

PLANS

The Individual Work Plan is dropped because it never was a real plan, simply an extract from a Stage or Detailed Plan. The Detailed Plan is now called a Team Plan.

STAGES

There is a separate section in the official PRINCE 2 manual to explain stages, though there is no difference in their concept to PRINCE Version 1.

PRODUCTS

PRINCE 2 is still product-based. The official PRINCE 2 manual gives Product Outlines for all management products. A Product Outline is a Product Description without 'Format', 'Quality Method' or 'Responsible' sections. Tailoring is needed to turn an outline into a Product Description. In line with the methodology's move away from its former IT concentration, the Product Descriptions for technical products are no longer offered.

PROGRAMME MANAGEMENT

There is now a firm link between projects and programmes. Programmes are explained, together with their relationships to projects. Throughout the methodology there are reminders of the possible impact of programme decisions on projects and vice versa.

3 | PRINCE Processes

PRINCE is a process-based methodology. It has eight processes which describe the steps to take from the inception of a project to its close.

The steps need to be studied and tailored to the specific project. In large projects for totally new products, all the steps may be required. But in a small project, or one enhancing a product which already exists, only one or two steps of a process may be required. Each process needs to be considered and judged on its merit for the particular project circumstances. To help the user, each process begins by answering the question on why it is needed, what it is trying to achieve.

The eight processes are:

- Start Up the Project
- Initiate the Project
- Direct the Project
- Control the Stage
- Manage Product Delivery
- Manage Stage Boundaries
- Close the Project
- Planning.

Each process consists of several sub-processes. Each sub-process has a number of steps. Figure 3-1 shows the processes and the passage of the main management and quality products between them.

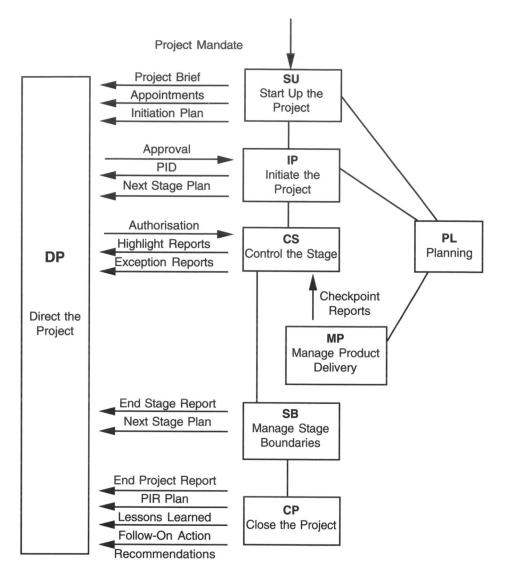

Project Mandate

Project Brief
Appointments
Initiation Plan

SU
Start Up the
Project

Approval
PID
Next Stage Plan

IP
Initiate the
Project

DP

Direct the
Project

Authorisation
Highlight Reports
Exception Reports

CS
Control the Stage

PL
Planning

Checkpoint
Reports

MP
Manage Product
Delivery

End Stage Report
Next Stage Plan

SB
Manage Stage
Boundaries

End Project Report
PIR Plan
Lessons Learned
Follow-On Action
Recommendations

CP
Close the Project

Figure 3-1. Process Overview

SU – Start Up the Project

TOP-LEVEL DIAGRAM

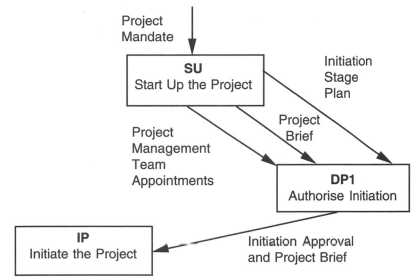

WHAT DOES THE PROCESS DO?

- Prepares (or confirms the existence of) terms of reference for the project (a Project Brief)

- Appoints the project management team

- Plans the Initiation Stage

- Advises interested parties, service providers (programme management, project support, Quality Assurance, accommodation) that the project is about to start

WHY?

- Controlled start to the project

- Establish who is to be involved

- Who is paying

- Who will say what is needed

- Who will make the decisions

- Who will do the work

How

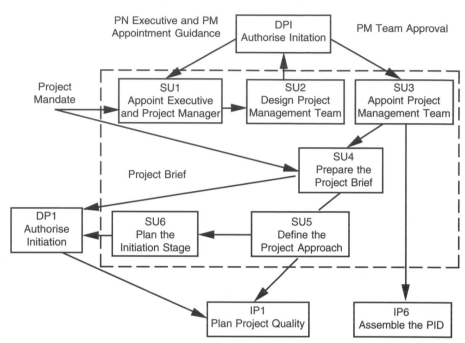

SU1 – Appoint the Project Board Executive and Project Manager

WHAT DOES THE SUB-PROCESS DO?

- Identifies who will hold the purse strings for the project
- Identifies an appropriate Project Manager
- Agrees job descriptions for the two jobs

WHY?

Before the project can begin, there is a need for someone to plan and prepare the first steps, and someone to approve the expenditure.

RESPONSIBILITY

The appointments are the responsibility of corporate or programme management. The agreement on job descriptions may be delegated by management to the Executive and Project Manager.

How	Navigation
Check for the presence of a Project Mandate (or Project Brief)	
Create a Project Mandate if one does not exist	Project Mandate Product Description
Identify the stake holders	
Identify the appropriate Project Board Executive	} Organisation
Appoint a suitably qualified Project Manager	
Draw up and agree job descriptions	Role descriptions

IN PRACTICE

'Project Mandate' is a general term to describe the trigger for the project. It may be a full specification of the problem, a brief, written request to 'look into' something or 'do something about ...', or a verbal request. The tasks of the sub-process SU4 will be to turn this request (over whose format there may have been no control by the Project Manager) into a Project Brief, whose content is defined by PRINCE.

If the project is part of a programme (and in many other instances as well) all the appointments may be predefined. In such cases all that is left is to agree job descriptions. This should not be ignored as it establishes responsibilities as well as authority.

FOR SMALL PROJECTS

The person requesting the project may well be the one paying for it. If so, that person becomes the Executive without reference to any other body. That is provided that the person in question has the budgetary authority to pay for the project. If not, then the Executive would be the first manager above that person, who had sufficient budgetary authority.

SU2 – Design the Project Management Team

WHAT DOES THE SUB-PROCESS DO?

- Proposes the other Project Board members
- Discusses with the Project Board members whether they will need help to carry out their assurance responsibilities

- Designs any separate assurance roles
- Identifies candidates for any separate assurance roles
- Identifies any required team managers
- Identifies any project support requirements.

WHY?

The complete Project Management Team needs to reflect the interests, and get the agreement of, the users of the final product, those who will specify details of the required product and the supplier of that product.

Senior management must decide whether they want independent checks on their particular interests in the project as the project progresses, or whether they can do this verification themselves.

The Project Manager has to decide if any administrative support is needed, such as planning and control tool expertise, configuration management, help with specialist techniques.

RESPONSIBILITY

The Executive is responsible for the work of the sub-process, but is likely to delegate much of the work to the Project Manager.

How	Navigation
Design a Project Board with representation of the final users and the supplier, which is suitable for the criticality and size of the project	Organisation
Identify candidates for the roles	
Check out their availability and provisional agreement	
Check whether the Project Board members will carry out their own assurance responsibilities	
Identify candidates for any assurance functions which are to be delegated	
Check out their availability	
Decide if any project support will be required	
Identify resources for any required support	

In practice

The composition of the Project Board may have already been defined, particularly if the project is part of a programme.

If the project is part of a programme, the use of the programme's assurance and support functions may be imposed.

If the management of many different user areas are looking for Project Board representation, it may be more effective to form a user committee, whose chairman represents all their interests on the Project Board.

For small projects

It would be normal for Project Board members to carry out their own assurance. In very small projects the Executive and Senior User roles will often be combined. If a department is developing a product for its own use and all the project's resources are from that department, the Senior Supplier and Senior User may also be the same.

SU3 – Appoint the Project Management Team

What does the sub-process do?

- Appoints other Project Board members, any required assurance and project support roles.

Why?

After the Project Management Team has been designed, the appointments need to be confirmed by corporate or programme management.

The understanding by each member of the Project Management Team of the job's requirements, authority and responsibility needs to be documented.

How	Navigation
The Project Management Team design is presented to corporate or programme management for approval	
The Executive informs each Project Management Team member of their appointment	
The Project Manager discusses each member's job description with them	Role descriptions

IN PRACTICE

Each Project Management Team member signs two copies of the agreed job description. One copy is retained by the person concerned, the other copy filed in the project files.

FOR SMALL PROJECTS

There may be no need to get approval from any higher level of authority than the Executive. There may be no project support functions. If Project Board roles are to be amalgamated, it may be sufficient to use the standard role descriptions – if the people concerned are well-versed in the PRINCE methodology.

SU4 – Prepare the Project Brief

WHAT DOES THE SUB-PROCESS DO?

- Creates the Project Brief from the Project Mandate.

WHY?

To ensure that sufficient information is available for the Project Board to decide if there is an adequate business case to proceed with the project.

RESPONSIBILITY

The Project Manager is responsible for preparing the Project Brief.

How	Navigation
Compare the information available about the required project against the information required by the Project Board in order to approve project initiation	Product Descriptions
Advise the Project Board how long it will take to prepare for the project initiation meeting	
Gather any missing information	
Check the business case with the Executive	

IN PRACTICE

The Project Mandate will be of variable content and quality.

If the project is part of a programme, a complete Project Brief may have already been provided, thus rendering this sub-process unnecessary.

The Project Manager should remember that it is a responsibility of the Project Board, particularly the Executive, to produce the business case, not the Project Manager's.

The Project Manager should informally check out the draft Project Brief with Project Board members to ensure there are no problems before formal presentation.

FOR SMALL PROJECTS

There may be pressure on the Project Manager to 'get on with the job' and start with an incomplete Project Brief. This should be resisted as it opens up the possibility of disagreement later on what the project was supposed to do (scope). The Project Manager also needs to know how much the solution is worth in order to make appropriate judgements if changes occur later.

SU5 – Define the Project Approach

WHAT DOES THE SUB-PROCESS DO?

- Decides on what kind of a solution will be provided and the general method of providing that solution
- Identifies the skills required by the approach
- Identifies any timing implications of the approach.

WHY?

The project approach will affect the timescale and costs of the project, plus possibly its scope and quality. This information should be made available to the Project Board in deciding whether to initiate the project.

A check should be made that the proposed approach is in line with the customer's (or programme) strategy.

RESPONSIBILITY

The Project Manager is responsible for the sub-process, assisted by any appropriate project support and specialist skills.

How	Navigation
Identify any time, money, resource, support or extension constraints	
Check for any direction or guidance on approach from earlier documents such as the Project Mandate	Project Mandate Product Description
Identify any security constraints	
Check for any corporate or programme statements of direction which might constrain the choice of approaches	
Consider how the product might be brought into use and whether there are any problems which would impact the choice of approach	
Produce a range of alternative approaches	
Identify the training needs of the alternatives	
Compare the alternatives against the gathered information and constraints	
Prepare a recommendation	

IN PRACTICE

The customer needs to think very carefully about the approach. Preparation of the above information can avoid being pushed into an approach which is favoured by a supplier, but which turns out to have later problems for the customer, such as lack of flexibility or maintenance difficulties.

FOR SMALL PROJECTS

The question is equally valid for small projects. The pressure to start work on a solution may lead to pressure not to perform this sub-process, but this should be resisted.

SU6 – Plan the Initiation Stage

WHAT DOES THE SUB-PROCESS DO?

- Produces a plan for the Initiation Stage of the project.

WHY?

Preparing a document to get approval to start the project is important work.

It needs planning, and since initiation will consume some resources, the plan for it should be approved by the Project Board.

How	Navigation
Examine the Project Brief and decide how much work is needed in order to produce the Project Initiation Document	Project Initiation Document Product Description
Evaluate the time needed to create the project plan	Planning
Evaluate the time needed to create the next stage plan	
Evaluate the time needed to create or refine the business case	
Create the Risk Log for the project	
Evaluate the time needed to perform risk analysis	Management of risk
Create a plan for the Initiation Stage	Planning process
Get Project Board approval for the plan	Project Initiation Meeting

In practice

The Initiation Stage should be short and inexpensive compared to the cost and time of the whole project, say 2 or 3 percent.

The Project Initiation Document is an extension of the Project Brief to include details of the Project Management Team and risk analysis, plus a refinement of the Business Case and the Project Plan. The Initiation Stage Plan should show the effort and resources to generate the extra information and the plan for the next stage.

If informal communication with members of the Project Board is to be frequent during initiation, this can reduce the need for formal reporting.

For small projects

Initiation may only take a matter of a hour or two and therefore may not need a formal plan.

IP – Initiate the Project

Top-level diagram

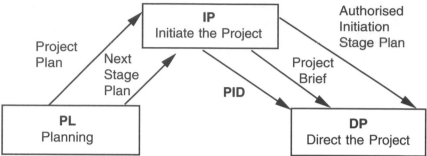

What does the process do?

- Gets the project off to a controlled start
- Lays the foundation for a well-planned and controlled project
- Identifies how success will be managed.

Why?

All parties with interest in the project should reach agreement before major expenditure starts on what is to be done and why it is being done.

How

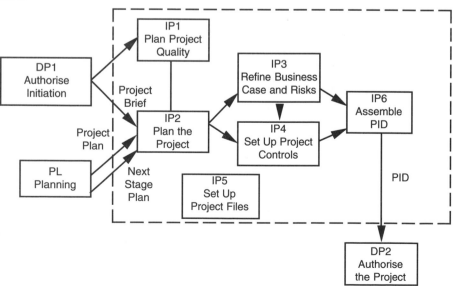

IP1 – Plan Project Quality

WHAT DOES THE SUB-PROCESS DO?

- Defines the quality expectations of the customer
- Takes the project approach and defines how the quality expected by the customer will be achieved.

WHY?

To be successful, the project must deliver a quality product, as well as meeting time and cost constraints. The means of achieving quality must be specified before work begins.

Quality work cannot be planned until the quality expectations of the customer are known.

The time and cost of the project will be affected by the amount of quality work which has to be done, therefore quality planning must be done before a realistic project plan can be produced.

RESPONSIBILITY

The Project Manager and those with assurance responsibilities are responsible for quality planning.

HOW	NAVIGATION
Establish the customer's quality expectations	Quality
Establish links to any corporate or programme quality assurance function	
Establish what the customer's quality standards are	
Establish what the supplier quality standards are	
Decide if there is a need for a quality assurance function for the project	
Identify quality responsibilities for project products in both the customer and supplier	Role descriptions
Establish how quality will be achieved	
Identify any required change control and configuration management procedures	Change control and Configuration Management

In practice

For in-house projects there may be no doubt about the quality standards to be used, but where customer and supplier are from different companies it is necessary to agree and document which standards will be used. In such circumstances it is important that the Project Manager specifies how the quality of the products from the supplier will be checked. Sensibly, this would be done by customer (user) involvement in the supplier's quality testing.

For small projects

Even if the customer leaves the quality checking to the developer, there should be customer involvement in specifying the testing environment and with what test situations the products should successfully cope.

IP2 – Plan the Project

What does the sub-process do?

- Produces the Project Plan

- Invokes the process SB1 (Plan a Stage) to produce the next Stage Plan.

Why?

As part of its decision on whether to proceed with the project, the Project Board needs to know how much it will cost and how long it will take. Details of the Project Plan also feed into the Business Case to indicate the viability of the project.

If the Project Board makes a general decision to proceed with the project, it needs to have more detailed information about the costs and time of the next stage before committing the required resources.

Responsibilty

The Project Manager is responsible for the products of the sub-process. There may be help from any project support appointed, and drafts of the plan should be checked with those carrying out assurance functions, particularly in terms of the quality work.

How	Navigation
Use the 'Planning' process to create the Project Plan	Planning
Review any project constraints	
Analyse project risks	
Modify the plan accordingly	
Decide on a suitable breakdown of the project into stages	
Invoke process SB1 (Plan the Next Stage) to produce the next stage plan	SB1 (Plan a Stage)
Check that both plans meet the requirements of the Quality Plan	IP1 (Plan Project Quality)
Check the plans informally with the Project Board	

IN PRACTICE

A Project Plan is always needed. The breakdown into stages may be encouraged by other considerations than just the project size. Examples might be risk assessment, major cash flow moments (invoice payment, invoice submission), and Project Board membership changes.

FOR SMALL PROJECTS

It may not be necessary to produce stage plans if the Project Plan can hold sufficient detail to allow day-to-day control. The Project Manager should decide at what point the inclusion of sufficient detail makes the plan too large to grasp in totality.

IP3 – Refine the Business Case and Risks

WHAT DOES THE SUB-PROCESS DO?

- Takes whatever outline Business Case exists for the project, plus the Project Plan, and creates a full Business Case for inclusion in the Project Initiation Document

- Carries out risk analysis for the project.

WHY?

Before commitment to the project it is important to ensure that there is sufficient justification for the resource expenditure. It is also important to have checked that the risks involved in doing the project are acceptable or that plans have been made to avoid, reduce or contain the risks.

RESPONSIBILITY

The responsibility for the Business Case rests with the Executive, probably with input of reasons from the user(s).

How	Navigation
If a Business Case was included in the Project Mandate, check if its circumstances and assumptions have changed	Business Case
Investigate the work reasons for the project with the user(s)	
Investigate the business reasons for the project with the Executive	
Quantify the benefits wherever possible	
Incorporate the costs from the Project Plan	
Perform risk analysis	Management of Risk
Modify the Project Plan to reflect any risk activities	
Prepare any contingency plans made necessary by the risk analysis	

IN PRACTICE

The Project Manager will normally have the work of pulling together the various inputs to the Business Case and performing risk analysis.

If the project is part of a programme, the programme will provide the overall Business Case. In such cases it may be sufficient in the Project Initiation Document to point to the programme's Business Case.

FOR SMALL PROJECTS

It is easy to start small projects without confirming that there are good business reasons for doing it. It is important, however small the project, to go through the exercise of justification. Otherwise, late in the budget year, it may be found that several unjustified projects have consumed the budget now needed for an important larger project.

IP4 – Set Up Project Controls

WHAT DOES THE SUB-PROCESS DO?

Establishes control points and reporting arrangements for the project, based on the project's size, criticality, risk situation, the customer's and supplier's control standards, and the diversity of interested parties.

WHY?

In order to keep the project under control it is important to ensure that:

- The right decisions are made by the right people at the right time
- The right information is given to the right people at the right frequency and timing.

RESPONSIBILITY

The Project Manager is responsible for establishing the monitoring and reporting necessary for day-to-day control, and agreeing the correct level of reporting and decision points for the Project Board to ensure management by exception.

HOW	NAVIGATION
Agree the stage breakdown with the Project Board	Stages
Agree the format of reports to the Project Board	Highlight Report Product Description
Agree the frequency of Project Board reports Establish the frequency of stage plan updates Establish reporting requirements from team(s) to Project Manager	} Project Controls
Check that there are sufficient risk and Business Case monitoring activities in the plans	Management of Risk
Set up a blank Lessons Learned Report to record useful points throughout the project	Lessons Learned Report Product Description

IN PRACTICE

If there are comprehensive control standards in existence it may be sufficient to point to the manual containing them, mention any which will not apply or detail any extra ones. The frequency of reports and controls should still be agreed for the project.

FOR SMALL PROJECTS

It may be acceptable to the Project Board that many of the reports are given verbally. But there should always be a formal initiation and a formal close.

IP5 – Set Up Project Files

WHAT DOES THE SUB-PROCESS DO?

Sets up the filing structure for management and quality records for the project. Filing or storage needs for the specialist products will depend on the type of products being produced.

WHY?

It is important to retain details of key events, decisions and agreements. These details may help in future project estimation, provide input to the Lessons Learned Report or provide a historical record of what happened, when and why. This is particularly important if relationships between customer and supplier turn sour because of, for example, disputes on scope or costs.

RESPONSIBILITY

The Project Manager is responsible. The work may be done by project support if such resources have been made available.

HOW	NAVIGATION
Create the Issue Log	Change Control
Create the Quality Log	Quality
Create project and stage files	Project Filing Product Description
Decide on any configuration management method requirements	Configuration Management

IN PRACTICE

By this time consideration must be given to any need for configuration management, particularly for the specialist products. There may be a standard method used by either the customer or supplier which is mandated for the project's products. If the project is part of a programme, the same configuration management method should be used.

The main question about configuration management is the need for it throughout the product's operational life.

FOR SMALL PROJECTS

A full-blown configuration management method may not be required, but consideration should be given to some kind of version control.

IP6 – Assemble the Project Initiation Document

WHAT DOES THE SUB-PROCESS DO?

Gathers together the information from the other IP sub-processes and assembles the Project Initiation Document.

WHY?

The Project Initiation Document encapsulates all the information needed for the Project Board to make the decision on whether to go ahead with the project or not. It also forms a formal record of the information on which the decision was based, and can be used after the project finishes to judge how successful the project was.

RESPONSIBILITY

The Project Manager is responsible for the assembly with the help of any appointed project support and the advice of those with assurance responsibilities.

How	NAVIGATION
Assemble the required information	Project Initiation Document Product Description
Decide how best to present the information	
Create the Project Initiation Document	
Distribute it to the Project Board, any others with assurance roles, and any others as directed by the Project Board	

In practice

Discuss with the Project Board whether it wants the Project Initiation Document to present all the information in full, or whether certain sections, such as Product Descriptions, job descriptions, can be referred to but not included.

For small projects

The Project Initiation Document should be a small document. The Product Descriptions appendix describes a Project Initiation Document Summary which can be used for small projects (and larger ones, too).

DP – Direct the Project

Top-level diagram

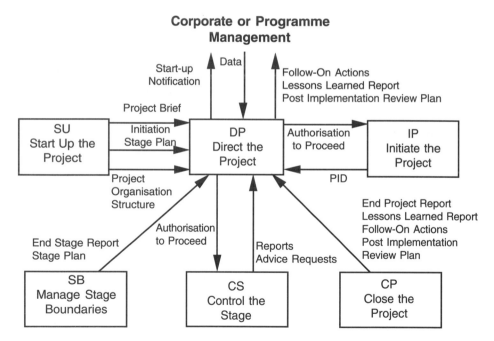

WHAT DOES THE PROCESS DO?

- Authorises initiation of the project
- Provides liaison with corporate or programme management
- Advises the Project Manager of any external business events which might impact the project
- Approves stage plans
- Approves stage closure
- Approves project closure
- Gives ad hoc advice and direction throughout the project
- Safeguards the interests of the customer, user and provider.

WHY?

Day-to-day management is left to the Project Manager, but the Project Board must exercise overall control and take the key decisions.

HOW

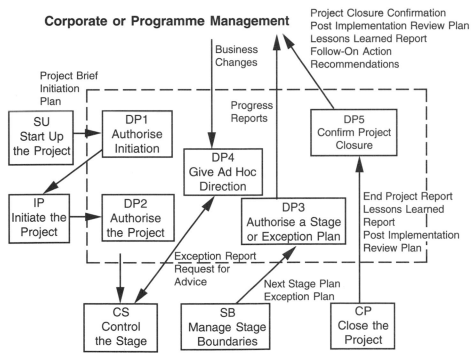

DP1 – Authorise Initiation

WHAT DOES THE SUB-PROCESS DO?

- Checks that an adequate Project Brief exists
- Checks and approves the Initiation Stage Plan
- Commits the resources required to carry out the initiation stage work.

WHY?

The initiation stage confirms that a viable project exists and that everybody concerned agrees what is to be done. Like all project work, the effort to do this needs the approval of the Project Board.

RESPONSIBILITY

The Project Board, based on information provided by the Project Manager and those with assurance responsibilities.

How	Navigation
Confirm the Project Brief, checking if necessary with corporate or programme management	Project Brief Product Description
Check the Initiation Stage Plan and approve it if satisfied	
Agree tolerance margins for the plan	Project Controls
Agree control and reporting arrangements for the initiation stage	
Commit the resources required by the plan	

IN PRACTICE

The Project Board should expect to be heavily involved in the initiation stage's work, and therefore should check on, and advise the Project Manager of, its own availability during the stage.

FOR SMALL PROJECTS

This can be done informally if the Project Board feel that that is suitable. The stage may be so short that no reporting during the stage is required.

DP2 – Authorise the Project

WHAT DOES THE SUB-PROCESS DO?

- Decides whether to proceed with the project or not
- Approves the next Stage Plan.

WHY?

The sub-process allows the Project Board to check before major resource commitment that:

- A reasonable business case for the project exists
- The project's objectives are in line with corporate or programme strategies and objectives
- The project's estimated duration and cost are within acceptable limits
- The risks facing the project are acceptable
- Adequate controls are in place.

RESPONSIBILITY

The Project Board with advice from those with assurance responsibilities.

How	NAVIGATION
Confirm that the project's objectives and scope are clearly defined and understood by all	
Confirm that the objectives are in line with corporate or programme objectives	
Confirm that all authorities and responsibilities are agreed	Role descriptions
Confirm that the business case is adequate, clear and, wherever possible, measurable	Business case
Confirm the existence of a credible project plan which is within the project constraints	Project Planning
Check that the plan for the next stage is reasonable and matches that portion of the project plan	
Have any desired changes made to the Project Initiation Document	

Confirm tolerance levels for the project and the next stage	Project Controls
Give written approval for the next stage (or not, if unhappy with any of the details)	
Arrange a date for the next stage End Stage Assessment	Project Controls

IN PRACTICE

The Project Manager should have been in regular informal contact with the Project Board to ensure that there will be no surprises when the Project Initiation Document is presented. If this contact has been maintained, the above list should be a quick confirmation.

If some minor item in the Project Initiation Document needs further work, but in general the Project Board is happy, approval to proceed can be given with the proviso that the corrective work be done – usually with a target date.

Very often the Project Board members are so busy with day-to-day duties that it is not easy to arrange an End Stage Assessment at short notice. It is better to plan the End Stage Assessment date well in advance, say, at the end of the previous stage.

FOR SMALL PROJECTS

The Project Initiation Document details may have been discussed and agreed informally over a (short) period of time. It may be sufficient for the Project Board to give the go-ahead when the last piece of information is presented without a formal full presentation. Approval to proceed should still be confirmed in writing as an important management document.

DP3 – Authorise a Stage or Exception Plan

WHAT DOES THE SUB-PROCESS DO?

- Authorises each stage (except initiation) and any Exception Plans which are needed.

WHY?

An important control for the Project Board is to approve only one stage at a time. At the end of one stage the Project Manager has to justify progress so far plus the plan for the next stage before being allowed to continue.

RESPONSIBILITY

The Project Board, based on information provided by the Project Manager and with advice from any separate assurance responsibilities.

How	Navigation
Compare the results of the current stage against the approved stage plan	
Assess progress against the project plan	
Assess the acceptability of the next stage plan against the project plan	
Review the prospects of achieving the business case	
Review the risks facing the project	
Get direction from corporate or programme management if the project is forecast to exceed tolerances or there is a change to the business case	
Review tolerances and reporting arrangements for the next stage	Project Controls
Give approval to move into the next stage (if satisfied)	

IN PRACTICE

The Project Board can stop the project for any reason, e.g. if the business case becomes invalid, project tolerances are going to be exceeded, product quality is unacceptable, or the risks become unacceptably high.

If the End Stage Assessment date was arranged some time ago and occurs before the actual end of the stage, the Project Board can give provisional approval to proceed based on one or more target dates being met to complete the current stage. If the stage finishes before the assessment, interim approval can be given to do some of the next stage work before formal approval is given. In such a case, the Project Board would clarify what work was to be done before the assessment, rather than give carte blanche to the Project Manager.

FOR SMALL PROJECTS

The decisions can be made informally, but the Project Board should still carry out the above activities.

DP4 – Give Ad Hoc Direction

WHAT DOES THE SUB-PROCESS DO?

- Advises the Project Manager about any external events which impact the project

- Gives direction to the Project Manager when asked for advice or a decision about a Project Issue

- Advises on or approves any changes to the project management team

- Decides on the actions to take on receipt of any Exception Reports.

WHY?

There may be a need for Project Board direction outside End Stage Assessments.

RESPONSIBILITY

The Project Board.

How	NAVIGATION
Check for external events, e.g. business changes, which might affect the project's business case or risk exposure	
Monitor any allocated risk situations	
Make decisions on any Exception Reports	Project Controls
Ensure that the project remains focused on its objectives and achievement of its business case	
Keep corporate or programme management advised of project progress	
Make decisions about any necessary changes to the project management team	
Make decisions on Project Issues brought to the attention of the Project Board	

IN PRACTICE

The key activity in this sub-process is deciding what action should be taken on Project Issues, including Requests For Change and Off-Specifications.

The procedure to be followed should have been agreed and documented in the Project Initiation Document.

This sub-process does not encourage general interference with the work of the Project Manager. The need for Project Board direction will be triggered by either a problem reported in a Highlight Report or an Exception Report, or an external event which it is monitoring on behalf of the project.

FOR SMALL PROJECTS

It may be sufficient for the Project Board and Project Manager to agree informally how to action a Project Issue as soon as it is documented.

DP5 – Confirm Project Closure

WHAT DOES THE SUB-PROCESS DO?

- Checks that the objectives of the project have been met
- Checks that there are no loose ends
- Advises senior management of the project's termination
- Recommends a plan for checking on achievement of the expected benefits.

WHY?

There must be a defined end point in a project in order to judge its success. The Project Board must assure itself that the project's products have been handed over and are acceptable. Where contracts (and money) are involved, there must be agreement between customer and supplier that the work contracted has been completed.

RESPONSIBILITY

The Project Board, advised by the Project Manager and any assurance responsibilities.

How	Navigation
The supplier gains acceptance from the customer that all the required products have been delivered and the acceptance criteria have been met	Project Controls
Checks that there has been a satisfactory hand-over of the finished product(s) to those responsible for its use and support	
Checks that there are no outstanding Project Issues	Change Control
Approves the Follow-On Action Recommendations and passes them to the appropriate group	
Approves the Lessons Learned Report and passes it to the appropriate body	
Approves the End Project Report	
Releases the resources allocated to the project	
Advises corporate or programme management of the project's closure	
The Project Board disbands the project management team	

In practice

It is sensible for the Project Manager to obtain written confirmation from the users and those who will support the final product that they have accepted the outcome of the project.

For small projects

Not all the reports may be needed, but there should still be a formal sign-off by the Project Board to close the project.

CS – Control the Stage

TOP-LEVEL DIAGRAM

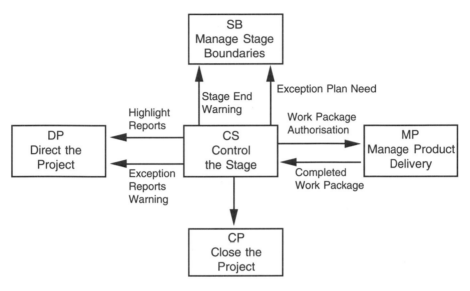

WHAT DOES THE PROCESS DO?

- Manages the stage between stage approval and completion.

WHY?

The production of the stage's products within budget and schedule and to the required quality requires careful monitoring and control.

How

See the diagram on the next page.

CS1 – Authorise Work Package

WHAT DOES THE SUB-PROCESS DO?

- Allocates work to be done to a team or individual, based on the needs of the current stage plan

- Ensures that any work handed out is accompanied by measurements such as quality expectations, delivery and reporting dates

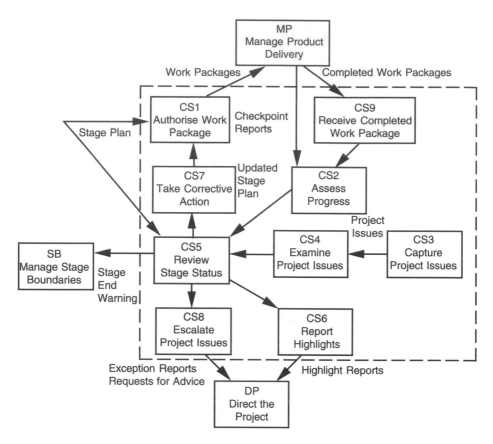

- Ensures that agreement has been reached on the reasonableness of the work demands with the recipient.

WHY?

The Project Manager must control the sequence of at least the major activities of a stage and when they begin. This ensures that the Project Manager knows what is being done by those working on the project, and that the stage plan correctly reflects this work.

RESPONSIBILITY

The Project Manager is responsible for the authorisation of work packages. The recipient of the work package must agree with the targets and constraints before the authorisation can be considered complete. If a Team Manager is receiving a work package on behalf of a team, this is covered by the process 'Managing Product Delivery' (MP).

How	Navigation
Ensure that there is a Product Description for the work to be done and that this is complete	Product Description
Make up the work package	Work Package Product Description
Discuss the work package with the Team Manager	
Jointly assess any risks or problems and modify the work package as necessary	
Ensure sufficient resources are available for the work	
Record the agreement of the Team Manager	
Complete a Work Package Authorisation	Work Package Authorisation Product Description
Update the stage plan with any adjustments made as part of the agreement	

IN PRACTICE

This structure should be used formally with appropriate documentation of both the work package and the Team Manager's agreement to its targets if the Team Manager represents a different company. In such cases it is sensible to specifically refer to the manner of work allocation in the contract.

If the stage plan is merely a summary of the start and finish times of major deliverables from a number of teams, there would be a work package for each of these major deliverables. In the quality method of the relevant Product Description should be definitions of who will check the product on behalf of the Project Manager (and/or Project Board) and at which points in the product's development.

If a Team Manager uses third parties to deliver any sub-products within a work package, it is recommended that this is also handled in the same way, i.e. as a Work Package Authorisation between the Team Manager and the third party.

The same structure can be used if the work is being allocated to an individual, rather than a team, but it can be done less formally.

FOR SMALL PROJECTS

The process can be followed in an informal way, but the Project Manager should consider if any record is needed for any later appraisal of an individual's performance. Where the Project Manager is also personally performing the work, the sub-process should not be needed.

CS2 – Assess Progress

WHAT DOES THE SUB-PROCESS DO?

- Updates the stage plan to reflect actual progress and effort expended.

WHY?

In order to control the stage and make sensible decisions on what, if any, adjustments need to be made, it is necessary to gather information on what has actually happened and be able to compare this against what was planned.

RESPONSIBILITY

The Project Manager.

How	Navigation
Collect checkpoint reports	Checkpoint Report Product Description
Collect stage plan progress information	
Obtain estimates on time, cost and effort needed to complete work which is in progress	
Check whether sufficient resources are available to complete the work as now estimated	
Check the feedback on quality activities	Quality Log
Update the stage plan with the information	
Note any potential or real problems	

IN PRACTICE

According to the size and environment of the project, the Checkpoint Reports may be written or verbal.

In fixed-price contracts the Project Manager may not be interested in gathering in the costs or remaining effort of team work, just the estimated completion date.

FOR SMALL PROJECTS

The Checkpoint Reports may be verbal.

CS3 – Capture Project Issues

WHAT DOES THE SUB-PROCESS DO?

- Captures, logs and categorises new Project Issues.

WHY?

At any time during the project a problem may occur, a change may be requested or the answer to a question sought. If these are missed, it may mean that the project fails to deliver what is required or runs into some other trouble which could have been foreseen, had the issue been noted at the time it arose. There must be a process to capture these so that they can be presented for the appropriate decision and answer.

RESPONSIBILITY

The Project Manager is responsible. If the project warrants it, help may be given by a project support function.

How	Navigation
The Project Manager ensures that all possible sources of issue are being monitored	
New issues are entered on the Issue Log	Issue Log Product Description
	Change Control procedure

IN PRACTICE

A site may have a well-established and successful procedure for handling all changes, and this can be used in conjunction with PRINCE. A check should be made to ensure that the procedure covers not only requests to change the specification, but potential failure to meet the specification, potential deviations from objectives or plans, and questions about some aspect of the project which require an answer.

FOR SMALL PROJECTS

Requests to change or failures on the part of the supplier still need to be documented as part of the audit trail of the project.

CS4 – Examine Project Issues

WHAT DOES THE SUB-PROCESS DO?

- Analyses each new issue and recommends a course of action
- Reviews each open issue for any change to its circumstances or impact and potentially makes a new recommendation.

WHY?

Having captured all issues in the sub-process 'Capture Project Issues' (CS3), these should be examined for impact and the appropriate body for any decision identified.

RESPONSIBILITY

The Project Manager together with any staff allocated assurance responsibilities.

How	Navigation
Assemble all pertinent information about the issue	Change Control procedure
Carry out impact analysis on the issue	
Update the Risk Log if the issue reveals a new risk or a change to a known risk	Risk Log Product Description
Prepare a recommended course of action	
Update the Issue Log with the impact analysis result	

IN PRACTICE

The Project Manager may ask a Team Manager or team member to carry out the analysis, depending on the expertise required. It may be necessary to analyse the financial impact as well as the technical impact.

FOR SMALL PROJECTS

The Project Manager may be able to carry out impact analysis as soon as the issue is presented and get a decision on the action to take, thus, in practice, combining the capture and examination sub-processes with the taking of corrective action or the escalation of the project issue to the Project Board for decision.

CS5 – Review Stage Status

WHAT DOES THE SUB-PROCESS DO?

- Provides a regular re-assessment of the status of the stage
- Triggers new work
- Triggers corrective action for any problems.

WHY?

It is better to check the status of a stage on a regular basis and take action to avoid potential problems, rather than have problems come as a surprise and then have to react to them.

RESPONSIBILITY

The Project Manager, who may seek guidance from the Project Board ('Escalate Project Issues' (CS8)).

HOW	NAVIGATION
Review progress against the stage plan	
Review resource and money expenditure	
Review the impact of any implemented Project Issues on stage and project plans	Change Control procedure
Assess if the stage and project will remain within tolerances	Controls (tolerances)
Check the continuing validity of the business case	
Check for changes in the status of any risks	Management of risk
Check for any changes external to the project which may impact it	

In practice

The sub-process should be viewed as one which is happening continuously throughout a stage, rather than one which is done, say, every two weeks. Each activity may not need to be done each day, but the Project Manager should ensure that there are sufficient monitoring points (and people allocated to do them) to keep a continuous check. This does not mean that there should always be an instant change of plan in reaction to each slight deviation, but maybe an extra monitoring point, a forecast of the potential impact if the situation were to get worse and a tolerance setting at which to trigger remedial work. A change which affects the business case or the risk situation may come at any time. As well as trying to identify such a change as it occurs, it is useful to review the assumptions on which the business case and risks are based on a formal, regular basis.

The Project Manager may seek guidance on any issue from the Project Board, and should always do so if there is a threat to the stage or project tolerances.

For small projects

These activities are still required. The Project Manager should make a decision about their frequency according to the project situation and environment.

CS6 – Report Highlights

What does the sub-process do?

- Produces Highlight Reports for the Project Board.

Why?

The Project Board needs to be kept informed of project progress if it is to exercise proper control over the project. Rather than have regular progress meetings, PRINCE recommends reports at regular intervals between assessments at the end of each stage. The frequency of the reports is decided by the Project Board.

Responsibility

The Project Manager.

How	Navigation
Collate the information from any Checkpoint Reports made since the last Highlight Report	'Manage Product Delivery' (MP)
Identify any significant stage plan revisions made since the last report	'Assess Progress' (CS2)
Identify any current or potential risks to the business case	
Assess the Issue Log for any potential problems which require Project Board attention	
Identify any change to other risks	Management of Risk
Report a summary of this information to the Project Board	Highlight Report

In practice

Input should come from process CS4, 'Examine Project Issues'.

The Highlight Report is a formal means of giving a progress update from the Project Manager to the Project Board. It can be used to bring to the Project Board's attention any failing in resources not under the direct control of the Project Manager and to give early warning of any potential problems which with the Project Board's attention can be avoided. The report should be kept brief in order to keep the attention of senior management to a minimum.

It does not prevent informal contact between the Project Manager and the Project Board if there is an urgent need for information to be passed or advice sought.

For small projects

The Highlight Report need not be in writing if the Project Board agrees to a verbal one.

CS7 – Take Corrective Action

What does the sub-process do?

- Within the limits of the tolerance margins established by the Project Board, the Project Manager takes action to remedy any problems which arise.

Why?

Failing to take action when the project is drifting away from the stage plan invites loss of control.

Responsibility

The Project Manager assisted by any project support and assurance staff appointed.

How	Navigation
Ensure that the situation is recorded in a Project Issue	Change Control
Ensure that all necessary information about the problem is available	
Identify action options	
Evaluate the effort and cost of the options and the impact of the options on the stage and project plans, business case and risks.	
Select the most appropriate option	
Assess whether it will keep the plans within tolerances	
EITHER implement the corrective actions and update the stage plan, if the work is within tolerances	
OR, where it would take the plan beyond tolerance margins, advise the Project Board	'Escalate Project Issues' (CS8)

In practice

The situation leading to the need to take corrective action should be formally recorded as part of the project audit trail, and the Issue Log is the easiest and most available means of doing this. Many of the reasons for corrective action will be Project Issues raised by other people.

For small projects

It is still important to log why plans were changed.

CS8 – Escalate Project Issues

WHAT DOES THE SUB-PROCESS DO?

- Gives the Project Board advance warning of situations which threaten the stage or project tolerances or the project's ability to meet its objectives.

WHY?

The tolerance levels are a major control feature for the Project Board. They are a major contributory factor to the Project Board's ability to manage by exception. The Project Board knows that if there is any threat to the tolerances, it will be alerted by the Project Manager by this sub-process.

RESPONSIBILITY

The Project Manager.

How	Navigation
Carry out a full impact analysis of the situation	'Take Corrective Action' (CS7)
Identify options	
Select a recommended option	
Supply an Exception Report to the Project Board	Exception Report Product Description and 'Give Ad Hoc Direction' (DP4)

IN PRACTICE

The Project Board's response may lead to either the sub-process CS7, 'Take Corrective Action', if the Project Board decides on action which keeps the plans within tolerances, or sub-process SB6, 'Produce an Exception Plan', if the decision is to change tolerances or products expected.

The exception situation may be good news, not necessarily bad news. The Project Board should still be informed.

FOR SMALL PROJECTS

The Exception Report need not be in writing if that is acceptable to the Project Board. The Project Manager must decide if it should be documented for the purposes of an audit trail as to why changes were made or decisions taken.

CS9 – Receive Completed Work Package

WHAT DOES THE SUB-PROCESS DO?

- This balances with sub-process MP3, 'Deliver a Work Package'. It records the completion and return of authorised work packages. The information is passed to sub-process CS2, 'Assess Progress'.

WHY?

Where work has been recorded as authorised to a team or individual, there should be a matching sub-process to record the return and acceptance (or otherwise) of the completed product(s).

RESPONSIBILITY

The Project Manager, assisted by any appointed project support staff.

HOW	NAVIGATION
Check the delivery against the requirements of the work package	Work Package Authorisation
Obtain quality confirmation	
Check that the recipients have accepted the products	
Ensure that the delivered products are baselined	Configuration management
Document any relevant appraisal information	
Pass information about completion to update the stage plan	'Assess Progress' CS2

IN PRACTICE

This sub-process is an on-going one throughout the stage.

FOR SMALL PROJECTS

The formality of this sub-process will relate to the formality of sub-process CS1, 'Authorise Work Package'. Both will often be informal and brief.

MP – Manage Product Delivery

TOP-LEVEL DIAGRAM

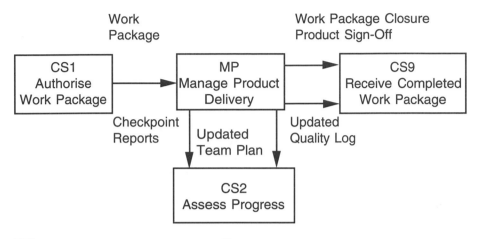

WHAT DOES THE PROCESS DO?

- Provides an interface between the Project Manager (using process CS, 'Control the Stage') and a third party

- Allows the Team Manager to:

  o Agree on the development and delivery of products with the Project Manager

  o Manage production of those products

  o Get acceptance of the finished products and sign-off for the work.

WHY?

The supplier may not use PRINCE, so this is a description of the necessary interface between the supplier and the Project Manager.

How

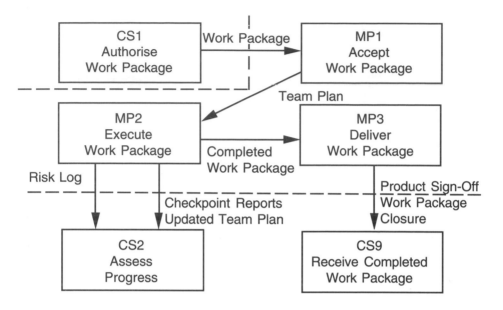

MP1 – Accept Work Package

WHAT DOES THE SUB-PROCESS DO?

- Covers agreement with the Project Manager on what is to be done
- Identifies any constraints
- Plans for the work to be done
- Ensures that there are sufficient resources to do the work.

WHY?

There must be a chance for the Team Manager (or individual) to negotiate the terms of a Work Package, rather than simply accept what the Project Manager believes can be done.

RESPONSIBILITY

Team Manager.

How	Navigation
Agree with the Project Manager on what products are to be delivered	} Work Package
Ensure that Product Descriptions are given for the required products	} Product Description
Agree on the standards to be used, the quality checks to be made and any constraints which apply to the work	
Understand who is to provide acceptance for the finished products	
Understand how hand-over of the products is to be made	
Confirm the Project Manager's reporting requirements	
Plan how, by whom and when the work is to be done	
Update the Risk Log with any new risks identified in planning the work	

In practice

Where third parties are involved, this sub-process should be carefully observed and checked against the contract to ensure proper safeguards for the supplier.

For small projects

The team members will probably work directly for the Project Manager, therefore this sub-process should be informal.

MP2 – Execute Work Package

What does the sub-process do?

- Covers the work involved in completing a Work Package

- Reports on progress

- Covers entry in the Quality Log of all quality checks carried out in performing the work.

Why?

How the Team Manager manages the work, what methods and tools are used is up to the Team Manager. This sub-process simply indicates the key activities, particularly those required to interface with the Project Manager.

RESPONSIBILITY

Team Manager.

How	Navigation
Allocate work to team members	
Monitor and control the work	
Produce Checkpoint Reports	Checkpoint Report Product Description
Ensure that any independent quality checkers are fully involved in the appropriate quality checks	Stage Quality Plan
Make entries in the Quality Log of the results of all quality checks carried out	Quality Log Product Description
Monitor any identified risks to the work	Management of Risk
Advise the Project Manager of any potential failure to meet the requirements of the Work Package	

IN PRACTICE

Even if the Team Manager is not using PRINCE, it would be sensible to have compatible recording and reporting procedures.

FOR SMALL PROJECTS

The Project Manager may do the work of this sub-process if there is only one team involved in the project.

MP3 – Deliver a Work Package

WHAT DOES THE SUB-PROCESS DO?

- Covers hand-over of the products of the Work Package
- Obtains acceptance for the products
- Advises the Project Manager of completion of the Work Package.

WHY?

Having formally received a Work Package in sub-process MP1, 'Accept Work Package', this sub-process allows the Team Manager to formally close the Work Package and get sign-off from the Project Manager.

RESPONSIBILITY

Team Manager.

How	Navigation
Handover the products of the Work Package	
Obtain sign-off for the products from those designated in the Work Package	Work Package Product Description
Advise the Project Manager of the completion of the Work Package	
Obtain any agreed confirmation from the Project Manager of acceptance of the completion	

IN PRACTICE

Acceptance of the products may involve one or more quality checks. It is a matter of choice as to whether those checks are considered part of this sub-process or MP2, 'Execute Work Package'.

FOR SMALL PROJECTS

Very little of this sub-process may be needed, if any at all.

SB – Manage Stage Boundaries

TOP-LEVEL DIAGRAM

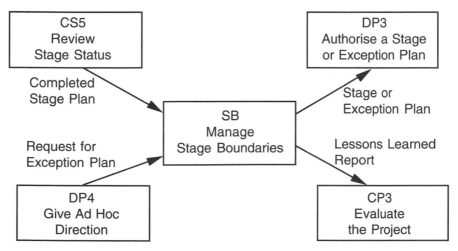

WHAT DOES THE PROCESS DO?

- Confirms to the Project Board which products planned to be produced in the current stage plan have been delivered

- Gives reasons for the non-delivery of any products which were planned (in the case of exception situations)

- Verifies that any useful lessons learned during the current stage have been recorded in the Lessons Learned Report

- Provides information to the Project Board to allow it to assess the continued viability of the project

- Obtains approval for the next stage plan or the exception plan

- Ascertains the tolerance margins to be applied to the new plan.

WHY?

The ability to authorise a project to move forward a stage at a time is a major control for the Project Board. There is therefore a need for a corresponding process to create a plan for the next stage and provide the information needed by the Project Board about the current status to judge the continuing worth of the project.

HOW

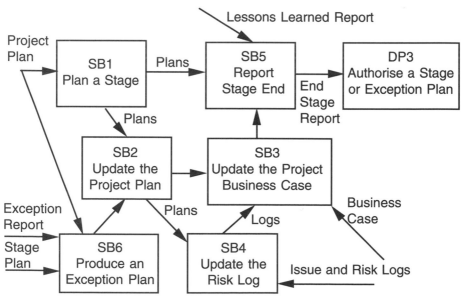

SB1 – Plan a Stage

WHAT DOES THE SUB-PROCESS DO?

- Prepares a plan for the next stage.

WHY?

In order to adequately control a stage the Project Manager needs a plan where the detailed activities go down to the level of a handful of days.

RESPONSIBILITY

The Project Manager.

How	NAVIGATION
Check the Project Approach for any guidance on how the products of the next stage are to be produced	
Check the Issue Log for any issues which will affect the next Stage Plan	
Use the common Planning (PL) process to create the draft plan	Planning (PL)
Document any changes to the personnel of the Project Management Team	
Discuss the draft plan with those who have assurance responsibilities	
Add any formal Quality Reviews and any other quality checks required for assurance purposes	
Identify (as a minimum) the chairman of each formal Quality Review	
Identify (ideally) the required reviewers for each formal Quality Review	
Ensure that the plan includes all required management products	
Check the plan for any new or changed risks and update the Risk Log	Management of Risk
Modify the plan, if necessary, in the light of the risk analysis	

IN PRACTICE

The Project Board should be kept informed of progress and any problems discussed and advice sought via the sub-process DP4, 'Give Ad Hoc Direction' before presentation of the Stage Plan.

FOR SMALL PROJECTS

The project may be small enough that the Project Plan contains sufficient detail to manage each stage, thus separate Stage Plans may not be needed.

SB2 – Update the Project Plan

WHAT DOES THE SUB-PROCESS DO?

- Updates the Project Plan with the actual costs and schedule from the stage which has just finished, plus the estimated costs and schedule of the next Stage Plan.

WHY?

As one stage is completed and the next one planned, the Project Plan must be updated so that the Project Board has the most up-to-date information on likely project costs and schedule on which to partially base its decision on whether the project is still a viable business proposition.

RESPONSIBILITY

The Project Manager.

HOW	NAVIGATION
Ensure that the current Stage Plan has been updated with final costs and dates	CS2, 'Assess Progress'
Create a new version of the Project Plan ready to be updated	Configuration Management
Update the Project Plan with the actual costs and dates of the current stage	
Update the Project Plan with the estimated costs, resource requirements and dates of the next stage	
Update any later stages of the Project Plan using relevant information available since the last update	
Check to see if events mean that the Project Approach has to be modified	SU5, 'Define the Project Approach'

IN PRACTICE

Text should be added to the new version, explaining why any changes have occurred. This is an important part of the Project Manager's 'trail' of documents covering the management of the project.

FOR SMALL PROJECTS

All the activity detail may be in the Project Plan with no separate Stage Plans. The Project Plan should be updated with the information described above.

SB3 – Update the Project Business Case

WHAT DOES THE SUB-PROCESS DO?

- Modifies the Business Case, where appropriate, on the basis of information from the current stage and the plan for the next stage.

WHY?

The whole project should be business-driven, so the Project Board should review a revised Business Case as the major part of the check on the continued viability of the project.

RESPONSIBILITY

The Project Manager and whoever has responsibility for the business assurance for the project.

HOW	NAVIGATION
Create a new version of the Business Case ready to be updated	Configuration Management
Review the expected costs in the Investment Appraisal against the new forecast in the updated Project Plan	
Review the financial benefits in the Investment Appraisal against any new forecasts	Business Case
Review the reasons in the Business Case and check that there has been no change or no new reasons have arisen	
Modify the new version of the Business Case in the light of any changes to forecast	

IN PRACTICE

The Business Case should be reviewed **minimally** at each stage end, but more frequently if the stages are long or the Business Case is at all borderline.

FOR SMALL PROJECTS

It should not be assumed that the Business Case is unimportant for a small project.

SB4 – Update the Risk Log

WHAT DOES THE SUB-PROCESS DO?

- Checks the known risks to project success for any change to their circumstances and looks for any new risks.

WHY?

Part of the assessment of the project's viability is an examination of the likelihood and impact of potential risks.

RESPONSIBILITY

The Project Manager collates the information on risks, but each known risk should have been allocated to an 'owner', the person best placed to monitor that risk.

HOW	NAVIGATION
Ensure that the Risk Log is up-to-date with the latest information on the identified risks	Management of risk
Ensure that any new risks identified in creating the next Stage Plan have been entered on the Risk Log	
Assess all open risks to the project, as defined in the Risk Log	
Decide if the next Stage Plan needs to be modified to avoid, reduce or monitor risks	
Create contingency plans for any serious risks which cannot be avoided or reduced to manageable proportions	

IN PRACTICE

An assessment of the risks should be part of the End Stage Report. The Project Manager should informally discuss any serious risks with the Project Board so that the risk situation and any extra costs incurred in reacting to those risks do not come as a surprise at the End Stage Assessment.

FOR SMALL PROJECTS

Continuous risk assessment and management are important to all levels of project.

SB5 – Report Stage End

WHAT DOES THE SUB-PROCESS DO?

- Reports on the results of the current stage

- Forecasts the time and resource requirements of the next stage, if applicable

- Looks for a Project Board decision on the future of the project.

WHY?

Normally the Project Board manages by exception and therefore only needs to meet if things are forecast to deviate beyond tolerance levels. But as part of its control the Project Board only gives approval to the Project Manager to undertake one stage at a time, at the end of which it reviews the anticipated benefits, costs, timescales and risks and makes a decision whether to continue with the project or not.

RESPONSIBILITY

The Project Manager.

HOW	NAVIGATION
Report on the actual costs and time of the current stage and measure these against the plan which was approved by the Project Board	End Stage Report Product Description
Report on the impact of the current stage's costs and time taken on the Project Plan	

Report on any impact from the current stage's results on the Business Case	Business Case
Report on the status of the Issue Log	
Report on the extent and results of the quality work done in the current stage	Quality Log
Provide details of the next Stage Plan (if applicable)	
Identify any necessary revisions to the Project Plan caused by the next Stage Plan	
Identify any changes to the Business Case caused by the next Stage Plan	
Report on the risk situation	
Recommend next action (e.g. approval of the next Stage Plan)	

IN PRACTICE

The Project Board should be aware of what will be in the End Stage Report before it formally receives it.

FOR SMALL PROJECTS

The report may be verbal, if this has the agreement of the Project Board.

SB6 – Produce an Exception Plan

WHAT DOES THE SUB-PROCESS DO?

- Prepares a new plan to replace the remainder of the current Stage Plan at the request of the Project Board in response to an Exception Report.

WHY?

The Project Board approves a Stage Plan on the understanding that it stays within its defined tolerance margins. When an Exception Report indicates that the current tolerances are likely to be exceeded, the Project Board may ask for a new plan which reflects the changed situation and which can be controlled within newly specified tolerance margins.

RESPONSIBILITY

The Project Manager.

How	Navigation
An Exception Plan has exactly the same format as a Stage Plan An Exception Plan covers the time from the present moment to the end of the current stage	Project Plans SB1 'Plan a Stage'

IN PRACTICE

Reasons for the exception situation can be many, such as:

- Work on approved Requests For Change cannot be done within current tolerances

- The stage cannot deliver all its products within the current tolerances.

FOR SMALL PROJECTS

There is the temptation not to re-plan, but only to 'remember' that changes have occurred. It is, however, important to advise the Project Board of any potential deviation beyond tolerances, to have a record that the Stage Plan was changed to accommodate the change and that the Project Board approved the new targets.

CP – Close the Project

TOP-LEVEL DIAGRAM

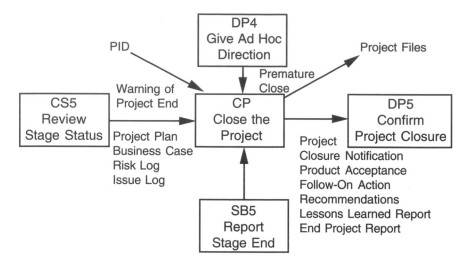

WHAT DOES THE PROCESS DO?

- Checks that all required products have been delivered and accepted
- Checks that all Project Issues have been dealt with
- Records any recommendations for subsequent work on the product
- Passes on any useful lessons learned during the project
- Recommends closure of the project to the Project Board
- Plans to measure the achievement of the project's Business Case.

WHY?

Every project should come to a controlled completion.

In order to have its success measured, a project must be brought to a close when the Project Manager believes that it has met the objectives set out in the Project Initiation Document.

How

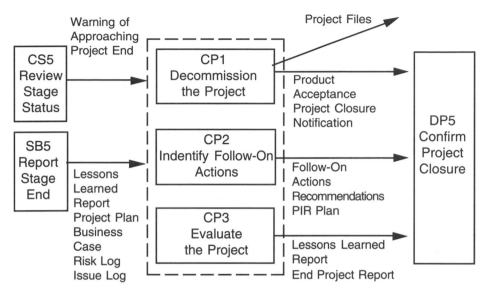

CP1 – Decommission the Project

WHAT DOES THE SUB-PROCESS DO?

- Gets agreement from the customer that the Acceptance Criteria have been met

- Confirms acceptance of the project's product from the customer and those who will support the product in its operational life

- Checks that all Project Issues are closed

- Prepares a notification for approval by the Project Board that the project's facilities and resources can be released

- Arranges archiving for the project files.

WHY?

The customer and supplier must agree that the project has met its objectives before the project can close.

There must be a check that there are no outstanding problems or requests.

Those who committed resources or facilities to the project should be advised of the impending project termination in order to consider their next allocation.

RESPONSIBILITY

The Project Manager and any Project Support staff assigned to the project.

How	Navigation
Check that all Project Issues have been closed	
Get the customer's agreement that the Acceptance Criteria have been met	SU, 'Start Up the Project'
Ensure that all products have been completed and accepted by the customer	
Ensure that, where applicable, those who will be responsible for maintenance and support of the products are ready to accept the project	Configuration Management
Complete and archive the project files	
Prepare notification to be issued by the Project Board that the project's resources and facilities are to be disbanded	

IN PRACTICE

This process may be abridged if it is brought to a premature close by the Project Board. There will need to be a carefully managed hand-over of the products between the project and operational and/or support staff unless one central group handles configuration management methods for both parts of the product's life cycle.

If any Acceptance Criteria have not been fully met, the customer and supplier may agree to record this as a Project Issue (Off-Specification) to be dealt with in a later project.

The final product may be handed over to a new third party to operate and maintain, and there may be contractual arrangements involved in the acceptance of the product.

FOR SMALL PROJECTS

Notification of the release of resources may be very informal, if required at all.

CP2 – Identify Follow-On Actions

WHAT DOES THE SUB-PROCESS DO?

- Identifies any work which should be done following the project

- Prepares a plan for when the realisation of the project's expected benefits should be checked.

WHY?

Any knowledge of unfinished business at the end of a project should be documented, checked with the Project Board and passed to the appropriate body for action.

RESPONSIBILITY

The Project Manager.

How	NAVIGATION
Check for any omissions in the product or suggestions on how to improve the product	
Ensure that the omissions and suggestions are recorded as Project Issues	
Check the Issue Log for any issues which were not completed or rejected	
Draw up Follow-On Action Recommendations	
Identify when measurement can be made that the product delivers its benefits and prepare a plan to carry out that measurement	Post Implementation Review

IN PRACTICE

The timing and arrangements for any Post Implementation Review should be discussed with the Project Board, particularly where there is an external supplier or support group.

Where the project is part of a programme, any recommendations for follow-on actions should be passed via the Project Board to the programme.

Where the project is part of a programme, there may be no requirement for a Post Implementation Review.

For small projects

There may be no requirement by the Senior User for a Post Implementation Review.

CP3 – Evaluate the Project

What does the sub-process do?

- Assesses the project's results against its objectives
- Provides statistics on the performance of the project
- Records useful lessons which were learned.

Why?

One way in which to improve the quality of project management is to learn from the lessons of past projects.

As part of closing the project, the Project Board needs to assess the performance of the project and the Project Manager. This may be part of the customer's appraisal of a supplier, to see if the contract has been completed, or to see if that supplier should be used again.

Responsibility

The Project Manager, project support and Project Assurance Team.

How	Navigation
Write the End Project Report, evaluating the management, quality and technical methods, tools and processes used	End Project Report Product Description
Examine the Risk Log and actions taken and record any useful comments	
Examine the Issue Log and actions taken and record any useful comments	Project Controls
Examine the Quality Log and record any useful comments	
Complete the Lessons Learned Report	Lessons Learned Report Product Description

IN PRACTICE

The Lessons Learned Report should have been updated throughout the project.

If there are suggestions that the Quality Management System used by the project needs modification, it should be made clear that such comments are directed to the appropriate Quality Assurance function.

FOR SMALL PROJECTS

The Project Board may not require an extensive End Project Report.

PL – Planning

TOP-LEVEL DIAGRAM

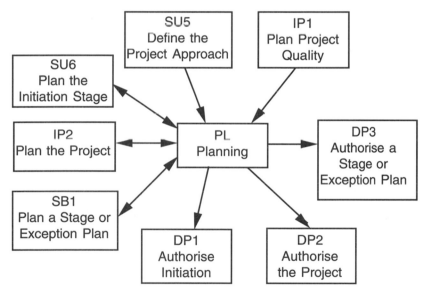

WHAT DOES THE PROCESS DO?

- Provides a common planning process to be used by all the processes which need to produce a plan.

WHY?

Planning is an essential part of project management. PRINCE offers a product-based planning process which can be applied to any level of plan.

To ensure that all plans are prepared in the same way and have the same composition, a common process is provided.

How

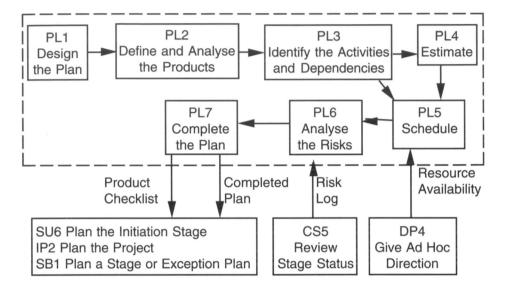

PL1 – Design the Plan

WHAT DOES THE SUB-PROCESS DO?

- Identifies the techniques and tools to be used to prepare the plan's products, the skills required, any planning tool to be used, the estimating method and how the quality plan will be met

- Identifies recipients of the plan.

WHY?

Planning is thinking about how to do a job before starting to do the job. In the same way, there needs to be some thought given to how planning will be done before beginning to plan.

RESPONSIBILITY

The Project Manager.

How	Navigation
Agree the format to be used for plans	
Decide what planning tool, if any, will be used	
Decide on the number of levels of plan needed for the project	Project Plans
Decide on the content and level of detail required for each plan level	
Decide how the estimation of effort will be done	
Identify the recipients of plan copies and their needs	
Agree with the Project Board the likely volume of Requests For Change and how they will be handled and funded	Change Control

In practice

This sub-process probably needs to be done only once early in the project.

The design must incorporate the decisions made in the sub-processes SU5, 'Define the Project Approach', and IP1, 'Plan Project Quality'.

For small projects

The work of the sub-process will be very brief, especially if there are company standards relating to tools and format.

PL2 – Define and Analyse the Products

What does the sub-process do?

- Identifies the major products to be produced by the plan
- Describes each major product, including its quality criteria
- Plans the required sequence in which the products are to be produced.

Why?

Identification of the products required is a good starting point for planning. Identifying the products whose delivery is to be planned leads naturally to the activities needed to produce and deliver those products. It is also possible to define the quality requirements of a product rather than an activity.

RESPONSIBILITY

The Project Manager with input and verification from the Project Assurance Team.

How	Navigation
Draw a hierarchy of the products required down to the level of detail appropriate to the plan	Product-based Planning Technique (Project Planning)
Make sure that the products include management and quality products as well as the technical ones	
Write Product Descriptions for all the products	
Get agreement from the Project Board that the Product Descriptions are complete and correct	
Draw a diagram showing the sequence in which the products must be created/delivered	

IN PRACTICE

The sub-process uses the product-based planning technique which is fully described elsewhere in this book.

FOR SMALL PROJECTS

The standard Product Descriptions in this book for management and quality products may not need modification, leaving only the Product Descriptions for the technical products to be done. It should only be necessary to write a small number of these.

PL3 – Identify the Activities and Dependencies

WHAT DOES THE SUB-PROCESS DO?

- Identifies the activities needed in order to produce the products

- Establishes any dependencies between the activities

- Identifies any dependencies on activities outside the plan's scope

WHY?

Planners may be more familiar with Work Breakdown Structures than

Product Breakdown Structures. Most planning tools are based on activities and this sub-process allows a transition to that mode of planning. Breaking a product down into the activities required allows the planner to go down to the level needed for control and defines the level at which Product Descriptions stop being written.

RESPONSIBILITY

The Project Manager.

How	Navigation
For each product on the Product Flow Diagram identify the activities needed to produce/deliver it	Product-based Planning Technique
Place the activities to produce a product in the order in which they need to be performed	
Check for dependencies on other products or activities in the plan and add these details	
Create a diagram showing the activities and their sequence	
Ensure that quality tests or checks are added	
Ensure that management products are added at the appropriate points	

IN PRACTICE

The activities can be added to the Product Flow Diagram where their sequence can easily be read.

This may be the point at which the planner begins to use a planning tool to create a planning network of all the activities.

After the network has been completed it may be necessary to add any management products which are to be produced on a time-driven basis, such as Highlight Reports.

FOR SMALL PROJECTS

It may be possible to estimate the time and resources required to produce a product from the Product Flow Diagram, in which case this sub-process may not be needed. But do make sure that the effort to check quality is built in.

PL4 – Estimate

WHAT DOES THE SUB-PROCESS DO?

- Identifies the resources, skill levels and time needed to carry out each activity.

WHY?

Estimation of resource requirements is a prerequisite to being able to schedule the activities and define how long the planned work will take and how much it will cost.

RESPONSIBILITY

The Project Manager. The job should not be done alone, but with at least one other experienced estimator.

How	NAVIGATION
Identify the skills and experience required for each activity	
Estimate the number of resources and the effort required to carry out each activity	
Identify any non-human resource requirements	
Ensure that resources have been allocated to quality checks and the production of management products	
Record any assumptions made in arriving at the estimates	Project Plans

IN PRACTICE

Product Descriptions can help produce estimates by detailing the composition of the products and the quality criteria to be met.

There are many methods of estimation, depending on the type of project. Alternatively, there may be a track record of doing the same or very similar activities which can be used as the basis of the estimates.

It is better to involve more than one person in the estimation, so that more experience is brought to bear and any undue optimism or pessimism on the part of one person can be balanced.

For small projects

There will be a temptation to have just one person do the estimation. This may not be a problem if the Project Manager is very experienced in the type of project. Otherwise, any estimate should be checked with someone who has that experience.

PL5 – Schedule

What does the sub-process do?

- Allocates available resources to activities

- Produces a draft schedule

- Revises the schedule in order to avoid over-utilisation and remove, where possible, under-utilisation of resources

- Costs the final schedule.

Why?

In order to see if the targets are achievable, the activities, now with estimated durations and resources, must be drawn out into a schedule to show when activities would begin and end.

All the work so far in creating the plan needs to be pulled together in order to find out the cost of the plan.

Responsibility

The Project Manager with assistance from the Project Board in terms of resource availability.

How	Navigation
Add resources to each activity	
Extend each activity to reflect the estimated effort	PL4, 'Estimate'
Produce a draft schedule based on the identified dependencies	PL3, 'Identify the Activities and Dependencies'
Smooth resource utilisation to remove over- and under-utilisation where possible	

Discuss the draft with the assurance responsibilities and ensure that their needs for quality checks are in the plan and resourced to their requirements	Quality
As a minimum ensure that the chairmen of any inspections or reviews have been identified	
Identify if the draft meets target dates and costs	
Discuss any problems with the Project Board and obtain a resolution	
Produce a final schedule and human resource costs	
Add any non-human resource costs	

IN PRACTICE

Ensure that the plan contains adequate control points.

Ensure that the plan covers the requirements of the Project Quality Plan defined in sub-process IP1, 'Plan Project Quality'.

Ensure that the plan follows the Project Approach defined in sub-process SU5, 'Define the Project Approach'.

Ensure that those with assurance responsibilities have examined the draft plan and identified where they want to see quality checks and the resources which should be involved.

FOR SMALL PROJECTS

The points above are still valid.

PL6 – Analyse the Risks

WHAT DOES THE SUB-PROCESS DO?

- Analyses the risk inherent in the draft plan
- Modifies the plan, where necessary, in reaction to the risks.

WHY?

It is foolish to undertake any venture without consideration of the risks involved. Before commitment to a plan, its risks should be evaluated and the plan modified where possible to avoid or reduce those risks.

RESPONSIBILITY

The Project Manager and the Project Assurance Team.

How	Navigation
Examine each activity, its timescale and dependencies and ask the question 'what could go wrong?' Ask the same question of each resource to be used Assess the likelihood and severity of each identified risk Modify the plan to remove, reduce or monitor the risks Enter each risk onto the Risk Log, together with the action taken	Management of Risk

IN PRACTICE

No plan should be put forward for approval until the inherent risks have been assessed.

FOR SMALL PROJECTS

It is still important to check the draft plan for risks.

PL7 – Complete the Plan

WHAT DOES THE SUB-PROCESS DO?

- Adds text to describe the plan and its creation.

WHY?

The complete understanding of a plan needs knowledge of the background, assumptions and risks involved.

RESPONSIBILITY

The Project Manager.

How	Navigation
Describe what work the plan covers	Stage Plan Product Description
Describe the planned approach	
Describe the quality control methods to be used	
Identify any plan dependencies on items outside the project's control	
Identify any prerequisites for the plan to succeed	
List the assumptions inherent in the plan	
List the agreed tolerances	
Identify how the plan will be controlled	
List the reporting arrangements	

IN PRACTICE

Tolerance margins must be agreed with the Project Board as part of its control of the plan. This should be done informally as part of the planning work.

FOR SMALL PROJECTS

It may be acceptable to the Project Board to talk it through most of the above items, but assumptions and tolerances should be documented.

4 | The PRINCE Organisation Structure

Why?

In any size of project it is important that all contributing parties agree on who is responsible for what, e.g.:

- The specification of what is required
- Project funding
- Decisions on the viability/continuation of the project
- Plans for what has to be done
- Day-to-day management
- The provision of resources
- The quality of the products
- Verification of the quality of the products
- Decisions on changing the scope or objectives
- Actually doing the work.

Key Points

If the project is to remain under control, project responsibilities have to be agreed at the outset of the project and not changed without everyone's agreement.

It is sensible for a company to have a standard pattern of project organisation which can be applied to all projects. On being appointed to a project role, staff will know what is expected of them, the basic organisation structure and what to expect from other roles. That standard should be sufficiently flexible that it can be applied to all sizes and types of project.

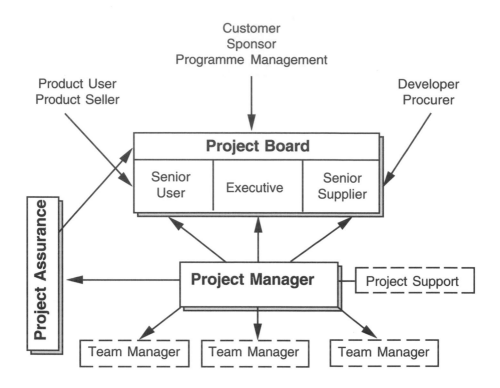

Figure 4-1. The PRINCE Project Management Team

The PRINCE Approach

In order to achieve the flexibility required, PRINCE describes the project organisation as a series of roles, not jobs. According to the requirements of each project, *a role can be shared by more than one person, or two or more roles can be combined.* The PRINCE project organisation can be used even for small projects without building up a top-heavy management team.

The PRINCE organisation structure allows:

- Key decision-making by senior management
- The delegation of day-to-day control to a project manager
- Decision-making by the project manager within limits set by senior management

- Negotiation between the Project Manager and one or more teams or individuals to carry out work

- Independent verification on behalf of the Project Board that the project stays on line to deliver what has been specified and meet the defined business case

- Administrative and technical support for the Project Manager, where needed.

Role Descriptions

THE PROJECT BOARD

The Project Board represents senior management's interest in the project. It is the key decision-making body, accountable to senior management for the success of the project. For medium or large projects it will normally be appointed by corporate or programme management. Its members must, therefore, be people who have the authority relevant for the size and criticality of the project to make 'go/no go' decisions on behalf of the project and commit the resources when a plan is approved. The limits of their authority should be established in the Project Brief.

It is likely that the Project Board members will be carrying out their Project Board functions in addition to a full-time job. The roles are therefore designed to be part-time. The emphasis is on management by exception. Controls and reports are geared to the need to keep their time commitment to the minimum, whilst allowing them to ensure that the project does not deviate from its objectives or plans.

The three roles identified in the Project Board represent:

- Who is paying for the project

- The people who will use the product when it is delivered

- Who will specify what is required

- Who will deliver the project's end products.

Or, to put it briefly, the Project Board is a platform where the customer or sponsor, the end user and the developer meet, negotiate and agree on project direction.

On small, internal projects the Project Board may be one person. Whether this is suitable can be judged after consideration of the responsibilities defined below.

Specific Responsibilities

This is a general list and should be tailored for each project.

RESPONSIBILITY	NAVIGATION
At the start of the project:	
Confirmation of Project Board appointments	SU3, 'Appoint the Project Management Team'
Agreement on the Project Manager's responsibilities and objectives	Project Manager role
Delegation of any project assurance roles	Project Assurance roles
Confirmation of project tolerances with the appropriate body of senior management	Project Controls
Specification of external constraints on the project, e.g., quality assurance or links with external bodies, programmes or projects	
Decision on whether to delegate some of its authority to sanction changes to the specification to a subordinate group	Change Control
Approval of an accurate and complete Project Initiation Document	Project Initiation Document Product Description
Approval of the next Stage Plan and commitment of the resources required.	
As the project progresses:	
Provision of overall guidance and direction to the project, ensuring that it remains within the specified constraints	DP4, 'Give Ad Hoc Direction'
Review of the project status at the end of each completed stage and approval of progress to the next stage	DP3, 'Authorise a Stage or Exception Plan'

Review and approval of any Exception Plans	
'Ownership' of responsibility to monitor one or more of the identified Project risks as allocated at plan approval time	Management of Risk
Approval of changes to the product specification	Change Control
Compliance with corporate or programme management directives.	
At the end of the project: Assurance that all expected products have been delivered satisfactorily	DP5, 'Confirm Project Closure'
Assurance that all Acceptance Criteria have been met	
Confirmation that, where appropriate, the operational and support groups are prepared to take responsibility for the product	
Approval of the End Project Report	End Project Report Product Description
Approval of the Lessons Learned Report and its passage to the appropriate group to ensure action on its recommendations	Lessons Learned Report Product Description
Decisions on any recommendations for subsequent modifications to the product (or other products) and the passage of these to the appropriate authorities	Follow-On Action Recommendations Product Description
Approval, where appropriate, of a Post Implementation Review plan and the transmission of the plan to the body which will be responsible for its implementation	Post Implementation Review Plan Product Description
Project closure notification to those bodies who supplied resources or facilities to the project.	

The Project Board's work is described in the DP process 'Direct the Project'.

The Project Board is accountable for assurance that the project remains on course to deliver the desired outcome of the required quality to satisfy the objectives and meet the Business Case defined in the Project Initiation Document. According to the size, complexity and risk of the project, the Project Board may decide to delegate some of this project assurance responsibility. This is discussed in the section on 'Project Assurance' later in the chapter.

Responsibilities of specific members of the Project Board are described below.

EXECUTIVE

The Executive role represents the customer or sponsor, usually the role holding the purse strings of the project.

The role is not shared in common practice, but with the advent of Private Finance Initiative, where the supplier is providing all or part of the funds, there may be a demand for part of the Executive's role to be taken by the supplier. In the main, though, the Executive represents the final owner of the product, and would normally come from the customer side.

The Executive is ultimately responsible for the project. The Executive has to ensure that the project represents value for money for the customer, ensuring a cost-conscious approach to the project, and balancing the demands of business, user and supplier.

Throughout the project the Executive is responsible for the Business Case.

Specific Responsibilities:

- Ensure that tolerance limits are set for the project in the Project Mandate, or at the latest in the Project Brief

- Approve the project Business Case

- Authorise project expenditure and set stage tolerances

- Brief corporate or programme management about project progress

- Organise and chair Project Board meetings

- Approve the End Project Report and Lessons Learned Report

- Recommend future action on the project to corporate or programme management if the project tolerance is exceeded

- Approve the sending of the notification of project closure to corporate or programme management.

The Executive is responsible for business assurance of the project, i.e. that it remains on target to deliver products which will achieve the expected business benefits, and that the project will complete within its agreed tolerances for budget and schedule. Business assurance covers:

- Validation and monitoring of the Business Case against external events and against project progress

- Keeping the project in line with customer strategies

- Monitoring project finance on behalf of the customer

- Monitoring the customer business risks to ensure that these are kept under control

- Monitoring any supplier and contractor payments

- Monitoring changes to the Project Plan to see if there is any impact on the project Business Case

- Assessing the impact of requests for change on the Business Case and Project Plan

- Informing the project of any changes caused by external events

- Monitoring stage and project progress against the agreed tolerance.

The Executive may delegate responsibility for some or all of the above business assurance functions if the project warrants it or the Executive has insufficient time to carry out these assurance duties. See the role of Business Assurance Co-ordinator under the heading 'Project Assurance' later in the chapter.

SENIOR USER

The Senior User represents the people who will use the final product, those who will specify the requirements of the end product. The Senior User leads user liaison with the project team and is accountable for monitoring that the solution will meet the user needs within the constraints of the Business Case. The Senior User role commits user resources.

There may be a need to share this role if several departments are to be involved in using the final product or whose work will be affected by the product. A sensible limit in such cases is three Senior Users. If there are more, consideration should be given to setting up a User Committee who appoint one or more representatives to sit on the Project Board as Senior Users. These would take the views of the committee to Project Board meetings and feed back information from the Project Board to the committee.

Specific Responsibilities:

- Ensure the desired outcome of the project is correctly and completely specified

- Make sure that progress towards the outcome remains consistent with the specified requirement

- Promote and maintain focus on the desired project outcome from the point-of-view of the end users

- Ensure that any user resources required for the project are made available

- Approve Product Descriptions for those products which will affect the users directly

- Sign off the products once these are completed

- Prioritise any proposed changes to the specification or acceptance criteria and contribute user opinions on Project Board decisions on whether to implement such changes

- Resolve any conflicts in user requirements and priorities

- Provide the user view on recommended follow-up actions at project closure

- Brief and advise user management on all matters concerning the project.

The assurance responsibilities of the Senior User are to confirm that:

- Specification of the user's needs is accurate, complete and unambiguous

- Development of the solution at all stages will continue to meet the user's needs and is progressing towards that target

- Impact of potential changes is evaluated from the user point of view

- Risks to the users are constantly monitored

- Testing of the product at all stages has the appropriate user representation

- Quality control procedures are used correctly to ensure products meet user requirements

- User liaison is functioning effectively.

Where the project's size, complexity or importance warrants it, the Senior User may delegate the responsibility and authority for some of the assurance responsibilities to the User Assurance Co-ordinator role, as described under the heading 'Project Assurance' later in this chapter.

SENIOR SUPPLIER

The Senior Supplier represents the developer(s) or procurers, the resources which will deliver the technical products of the project. In some environments the customer may share design authority or have a major say in it. If necessary more than one person may be required to represent the suppliers. If this happens, care should be taken not to allow the suppliers to outnumber or outvote the customer.

It is possible for the Senior Supplier role to be taken by the contracts manager for the customer. The key point is that the Senior Supplier appointed must be able to make commitments on behalf of the supplying party. A study of the Senior Supplier's responsibilities listed below will help clarify who the Senior Supplier should be.

This is the most difficult role for some to understand.

Specific Responsibilities:

- Agree objectives for supplier activities

- Make sure that progress towards the outcome remains consistent from the supplier perspective

- Promote and maintain focus on the desired project outcome from the point of view of supplier management

- Ensure that the supplier resources required for the project are made available

- Approve Product Descriptions for products on behalf of the supplier

- Contribute supplier opinions on Project Board decisions on whether to implement recommendations on proposed changes

- Resolve supplier requirements and priority conflicts

- Arbitrate on, and ensure resolution of, any supplier resource or priority conflicts

- Brief non-technical management on supplier aspects of the project.

The Senior Supplier is responsible for the technical integrity of the project. The technical assurance role responsibilities are to:

- Advise on the selection of technical strategy, design and methods

- Ensure that any technical standards defined for the project are met and used to good effect

- Monitor potential changes and their impact on the correctness, completeness and integrity of products against their Product Description from a technical perspective

- Monitor any risks in the technical and production aspects of the project

- Ensure quality control procedures are used correctly so that products adhere to technical requirements.

If warranted, some of this assurance responsibility may be delegated to a separate Technical Assurance Co-ordinator role. This role is described later in this chapter under the heading 'Project Assurance'.

PROJECT MANAGER

The Project Manager is given the authority to run the project on a day-to-day basis by the Project Board within tolerance limits laid down by the board. In a customer/supplier environment it is recommended that the Project Manager should come from the customer organisation.

There may be projects where the Project Manager comes from the supplier. In this case the customer may appoint a 'Project Director' or 'Controller' to be its day-to-day liaison with the Project Manager.

The Project Manager's prime responsibility is to produce a final product which is capable of achieving the benefits defined in the Business Case. This entails ensuring that the project produces the required products, to the required standard of quality and within the specified constraints of time and cost.

Specific Responsibilities:

- Manage the development and delivery of the required products

- Manage the project team

- Plan and monitor the project

- Work with any project assurance roles appointed by the Project Board

- Produce the Project Initiation Document

- Prepare any required plans in conjunction, where appropriate, with Team Managers, and the Project Assurance Team, and agree them with the Project Board

- Manage business and project risks

- Liaise with programme management (if the project is part of a programme) or any related projects to ensure that required products are neither overlooked nor duplicated

- Monitor overall progress and use of resources, and initiate corrective action, where necessary, within the tolerance limits defined by the Project Board

- Implement change control and any required Configuration Management procedures

- Report to the Project Board in the manner and at the frequency defined in the Project Initiation Document

- Liaise with the Project Board or its appointed Project Assurance Team to assure the overall direction and integrity of the project

- Agree technical and quality strategy with appropriate members of the Project Board

- Compile a report on any lessons learned about the project management and technical methods and tools used

- Prepare any recommendations for follow-on actions after the project close

- Prepare the End Project Report

- Ask the Project Board for any support and advice required for the management, planning and control of the project

- Be responsible for project administration

- Liaise with any sub-contractors.

TEAM MANAGER

This role is not mandatory. There may be only one team in a project, directly managed by the Project Manager. On the other hand the project may need several teams, each with specialised skills and knowledge. The Project Manager may find that it is beneficial to delegate the authority and responsibility for planning the creation of those products and managing the team(s) to produce those products. The Team Manager agrees with the Project Manager what work is to be done by the team, manages its performance and returns the completed products to the Project Manager. The Team Manager reports to and takes direction from the Project Manager.

The use of this role should be decided between the Project Manager and the Project Board at Project Initiation time.

The Team Manager may work for a third party which is not using PRINCE.

Specific Goals

- Receive authorisation from the Project Manager to create products (Work Package)

- Negotiate and agree the terms of the Work Package Authorisation with the Project Manager

- Prepare plans for the team's work

- Manage the team

- Take responsibility for the progress of the team's work and use of team resources, and initiate corrective action where necessary within the constraints laid down by the Project Manager

- Advise the Project Manager of any deviations from plan, recommend corrective action, and help prepare any appropriate Exception Plans

- Pass products which have been completed and approved in line with the Work Package Authorisation back to the Project Manager

- Ensure that any Project Issues arising from the Work Package are properly reported to the person maintaining the Issue Log

- Ensure the evaluation of Project Issues which arise within the team's work and recommend action to the Project Manager

- Liaise with any Project Assurance Team

- Attend any stage assessments as required by the Project Manager

- Arrange and lead team checkpoints

- Ensure that the quality of the team's work is planned and controlled correctly

- Ensure the maintenance of records of the team's work

- Identify and advise the Project Manager of any risks associated with a Work Package

- Manage specific risks as directed by the Project Manager.

PROJECT ASSURANCE

Project Assurance is the independent monitoring of project progress on behalf of one or more members of the Project Board. It may be done by the Project Board members themselves or they may delegate some or all of their assurance responsibilities to others who have more time or more appropriate skills.

The three major areas of assurance are:

- Business (monitoring the business case, business risks and expenditure)

- Technical (monitoring the use of standards and the quality of the products)

- User (monitoring that the end product continues to meet the user's specification throughout its development).

Project Assurance monitors the work of the Project Manager, Team Managers and team members. Project Assurance is independent of the Project Manager, therefore the Project Board cannot delegate its assurance responsibilities to the Project Manager.

PROJECT ASSURANCE TEAM

For those projects which wish to appoint staff to assurance roles, below are listed the three most common ones. For the sake of convenience in wording these responsibilities, those given assurance responsibilities in a project are called the Project Assurance Team in the rest of this manual. This applies even if the Project Board members carry out their assurance responsibilities personally. A member of the Project Assurance Team may be part-time, full-time or the role may be shared by several people.

Business Assurance Co-ordinator (BAC)

The main concern of a BAC is to monitor the business case and anything which might afect it. In a customer/supplier environment there may be different business cases for the customer and the supplier. In such cases both parties may wish to appoint a BAC, one to monitor each business case. The customer's BAC would normally report to the Executive and would be delegated some or all of the Executive's assurance responsibilities, as listed below:

- Validating the Business Case in the Project Initiation Document
- Monitoring the Business Case against external events and against project progress
- Keeping the project in line with company strategies
- Monitoring project expenditure
- Monitoring the business risks to ensure that these are kept under control
- Monitoring any supplier and contractor payments
- Monitoring changes to the Project Plan to see if there is any impact on the Business Case
- Assessing the impact of potential changes on the Business Case and Project Plan

- Informing the project of any changes caused by external events

- Monitoring stage and project progress against the agreed tolerance limits.

User Assurance Co-ordinator (UAC)

The main responsibilities of this role are to monitor the project's ability to deliver a product which meets the specification and quality requirements. The role represents the assurance interests of the Senior User. Any appointment should be made for the life of the project to give continuity. The assurance responsibilites are listed below. Any appointment should be to a person who has a sufficient level of authority not to be overruled by the Project Manager. Any disagreement between a UAC and a Project Manager should be taken to the Senior User to resolve.

The UAC assures that:

- Specification of the user's needs is accurate, complete and unambiguous

- Throughout the project a solution is being developed which will meet the user's needs

- The impact on the users of any suggested changes is evaluated

- Risks which would affect the users are constantly monitored

- The quality checking of the product at all stages has suitable user representation

- User liaison with the project is functioning effectively.

Technical Assurance Co-ordinator (TAC)

Basically the TAC carries out the assurance responsibilities of the Senior Supplier if these are delegated. But in a customer/supplier environment, the customer may also wish to appoint one or more people as TACs to technically assure the work the supplier or sub-contractors are doing. The Senior User and Executive may use an outside consultant as a TAC to monitor the technical aspects if they are unskilled in these areas. Similarly, if a company has an overall technical strategy, the strategy group may provide a TAC to one or more projects to monitor the design against their technical strategy.

A TAC may be appointed for the entire project, or different people may be appointed to the role at different times in the project according to the skills needed at that time.

Where an organisation has a separate Quality Assurance function, someone from that function may be appointed to an assurance role for each project. This could be either the TAC role or a separate role specifically designed for quality assurance.

The following responsibilities of a TAC are general and will need to be tailored to the needs of a project:

- Advise on the technical strategy to be followed
- Advise on the selection of design and development methods
- Advise on or confirm the suitability of technical standards for the project
- Confirm that development staff are trained in the chosen standards
- Ensure that the technical standards defined for the project are used to good effect
- Evaluate potential changes from a technical perspective against the Product Descriptions of the relevant products and assess the impact of such changes on the correctness, completeness and integrity of products
- Monitor any risks to the technical aspects of the project
- Ensure quality control procedures are used correctly so that products adhere to technical requirements.

PROJECT SUPPORT

This is another optional set of roles. They cover project administration, filing, acting as meeting scribe, meetings organiser, support tool expertise (such as planning and control tools), change control and configuration management. The last two are the most important areas.

Main Tasks

The following is a list of project support tasks. The Project Manager should consider if support is needed to carry out any of these tasks for the project.

In larger organisations there may be a separate configuration management group which provides this service to all products, whether being developed in a project or in their operational life.

Planning and Control

- Provide expertise in the planning and control tool(s) to be used
- Collect actuals data and forecasts
- Update plans.

Configuration Management

- Administer change control
- Set up and maintain project files
- Establish a configuration management method for the project
- Establish document control procedures
- Copy and distribute products.

(A full Configuration Librarian role description is given below.)

Administration

- Administer the Quality Review process
- Administer Project Board meetings
- Assist with the compilation of Reports.

CONFIGURATION LIBRARIAN

Major Functions

- Planning, monitoring and reporting on Configuration Management (CM) aspects.
- Acting as the focal point for Configuration Control.

Role Description

- Assist the Project Manager to prepare the Configuration Management Plan.
- Help the Project Manager to create CM structure and identification scheme.

- Assist in the identification of Configuration Items (CI).

- Create Configuration Item Description Records (CIDR). In PRINCE terms these may be called Product Descriptions.

- Ensure that the structural relationship between products is known.

- Archive superseded Product Descriptions.

- Accept and record receipt of Submission Request Forms with new or revised products into the CM library.

- Act as custodian for master copies of all project products as defined in the CM plan.

- Issue product copies for review, change, correction or information.

- Maintain copy holder information for both human and machine readable products.

- Notify holders of any changes to their copies.

- Maintain logs for Project Issues.

- Monitor all Project Issue documents and ensure they are re-submitted to the CM library after any authorised change.

- Copy the original author of a Project Issue document whenever its status changes.

- Establish a method which provides a link between a product and the record of its quality check in the Quality File.

- Document a product's history so that traceability is assured if a product structure is changed during its life cycle. Wherever possible the product structure should not be changed other than to include additional items.

- Assist staff to assess the impact of a change to a product.

- Produce Configuration Status Accounting reports.

- Assist in conducting Configuration Audits.

- Create baseline records as required.

- Produce release packages.

Link to Controls

The diagram in Figure 4-2 links the various roles in the Project Management Team with the PRINCE controls which those roles apply and the roles which supply the information for those controls.

Programme Management

A programme is a major undertaking, usually over a considerable time, which has many separate parts, all of which contribute to the aims of the programme. For example, a borough council will have a programme of road improvements. Many roads will be affected. Each individual improvement will be a project in its own right. What are the links between a programme and its projects?

There will be a business case for the programme. The business case for each project must relate to the business case of the programme. It will often be creating one or more products which will help achieve the expected benefits of the programme. The entire justification for a project may be that it is contributing to the programme's business case.

There will be a plan for the programme which will indicate when the individual projects start, their expected duration and cost. This information is handed down to the project in the Project Brief. The individual project plan refines these estimates and is fed back to those responsible for the programme plan. Similarly, when the project plan is updated at each stage end, details of the update are sent to the programme.

Changes made to the specification of a project may have an impact on other projects in the programme and on the programme budget. There needs to be a close link between project and programme change control. Often change control for all projects in a programme are co-ordinated at the programme level to avoid one project getting out of step with the others.

Tolerance limits on time and money will have been set for the programme. The management of the programme have to allocate part of those tolerances to each project in the programme.

Just as the Project Manager reports on project progress to the Project Board, the Project Board has to report on progress to the management of the programme. Just as a Team Manager confirms the successful hand-

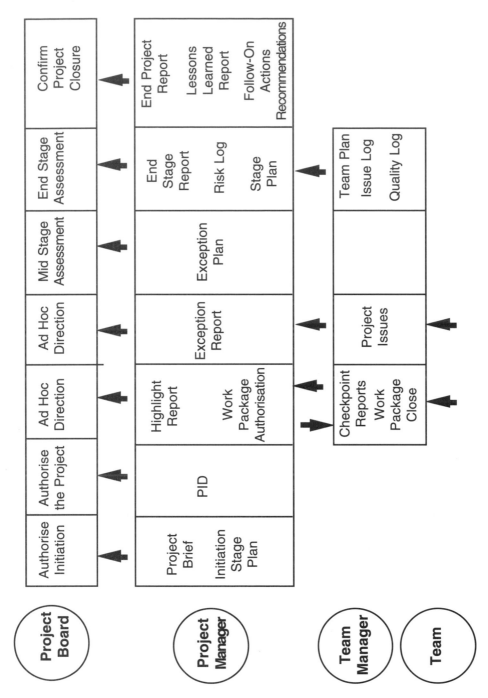

Figure 4-2. The PRINCE organisation structure links to controls

over of a completed Work Package to the Project Manager, the Project Board has to confirm the results of the project to the programme management at project closure.

Figure 4-3 shows the organisation of a programme management team and where there may be links with a project management team.

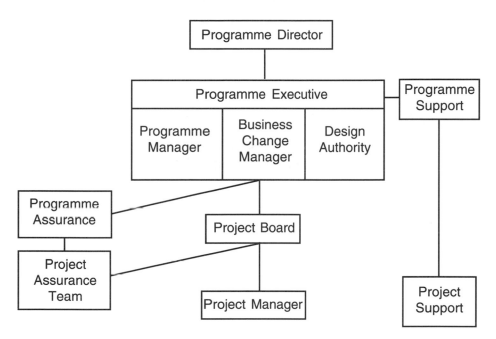

Figure 4-3. Programme Management Organisation and the links with a Project Management Team

PROGRAMME DIRECTOR

The Programme Director is in charge of the programme. The role is responsible for:

- Establishing the programme and identifying the individual projects
- Individual Project Board appointments
- Monitoring programme progress
- Ensuring the aims of the programme and projects continue to be aligned with evolving business needs
- The realisation of the programme benefits.

The Programme Director is responsible for establishing each Project Board. Having appointed the project Executive, the Programme Director may delegate the appointment of the remainder of the Project Board to the project Executive. Whichever option is followed, thought must be given to both the need for programme representation on each project and the need for the project to be seen to be locally owned, thus promoting the adoption of the project's output by the customer and users.

If the Programme Director has already appointed the Project Board, this removes the need to design and appoint the Project Board, part of the process 'Start Up a Project' (SU).

PROGRAMME EXECUTIVE

Authority for the day-to-day management of a programme is delegated by the Programme Director to the Programme Executive.

At the programme level assurance is carried out by two roles within the Programme Executive; the Business Change Manager and the Design Authority.

Members of the Programme Executive may share attendance at individual Project Board meetings between them.

Programme Manager

The Programme Manager is the key management link between programme and projects, giving general direction to the Project Managers.

The Programme Manager co-ordinates the programme's portfolio of projects on behalf of the Programme Director on a day-to-day basis, focusing on any changes which affect the programme.

The Programme Manager is responsible for ensuring the management of programme-related risks, particularly those associated with inter-dependencies between projects.

The Programme Manager may take the Executive role on the Project Board or represent the programme at Project Board meetings without taking a specific Project Board role.

Business Change Manager

The Business Change Manager represents the Programme Director's interests in the final outcome of the programme, is responsible for the final Business Case and for funding the programme work. The word 'Change' in the title is the change to the customer's way of doing business which will be brought about by the programme. The role must ensure that managers and staff in the business area(s) affected by the programme are informed and involved throughout the life of the programme, and are prepared to take advantage of the changed operational business environment.

The Business Change Manager may take on the role of Senior User.

Design Authority

The Design Authority should ensure that the designs created by the projects which are part of the portfolio are consistent and the interfaces between projects are designed consistently. The Design Authority also ensures that all project designs comply with the policies and standards of the programme.

Programme Representation in Projects

In order to maintain good liaison with and control over the individual projects, programme management may have one or more representatives on each Project Board. Similarly, there may be a Programme Assurance Team which carries out assurance duties on each project on behalf of programme management. These may remain separate to the Project Assurance Team or take a role on each Project Assurance Team.

There may be support at programme level for such items as change control and configuration management, or expertise in planning and control methods and software. If so, these should have control over the same work being done at project level to ensure consistency and co-ordination.

5 | Project Plans

Why?

A plan:

- Shows whether the target is achievable
- Shows what resources are needed to accomplish the work
- Shows how long the work will take
- Shows who is to do what and when
- Gives a basis for assessing the risks involved in the work
- Provides the base against which progress can be measured
- Provides the information on the Project Manager's intentions to be communicated to those concerned
- Can be used to gain the consent and commitment of those who have to contribute in some way.

What does a Plan do?

A plan defines:

- The steps required in order to achieve a specified target
- The sequence of those steps
- Any interdependencies between them
- How long each step is estimated to take
- When the steps take place
- Who will carry out the steps
- Where controls are to be applied.

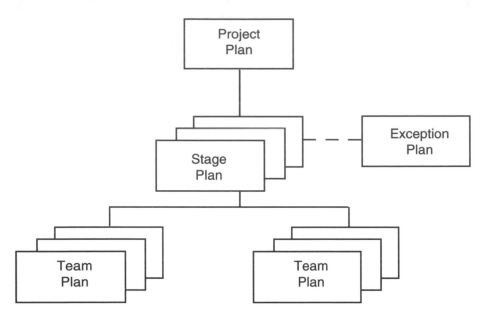

Figure 5-1. PRINCE Plan Levels

Levels of Plan

PRINCE offers a flexible hierarchy of plans to match the needs of the Project Board, the Project Manager, and Team Managers. This hierarchy is adjusted to the needs of a specific project.

Each level of plan has the same format. Only the amount of detail differs.

PROJECT PLAN

The Project Plan is a major control document for the Project Board. It is produced during the Initiation Stage as part of the Project Initiation Document on which the Project Board bases its decision on whether to commit to the project. At the end of each stage the Project Manager updates the Project Plan with the latest information and the Project Board uses this information as part of its judgement on whether to continue with the project. The Project Plan is the only mandatory plan in the project.

The Project Plan is a high level plan, showing the timing of the production of the major products, the stage divisions and the resources needed. If the project is a very small one, the Project Manager may decide to combine the Stage and Project Plans.

Stage Plan

The Stage Plan is the major planning and control aid of the Project Manager. It is produced immediately before a stage and covers that stage in the detail necessary to give the Project Manager day-to-day control of progress. This entails breaking down each product to a level where its production is a small number of days, say less than ten. This allows feedback to the Project Manager on any small deviation where action can be taken before the situation becomes serious.

Team Plan

If there is more than one team working on the stage, it may be sensible to have a detailed plan for the work of each team. This would be the case if sub-contractors were doing the work. In such cases, the Stage Plan might be a summary of the Team Plans, showing the timings of product work, delivery and interfaces.

Team Plans are based on the Work Packages agreed between Project Manager and Team Manager.

Exception Plan

An Exception Plan is only required if a Stage Plan is forecast to exceed its tolerances. It would normally follow the issue of an Exception Report from the Project Manager to the Project Board. (Remember that the Project Board may instead decide to close a project prematurely.) An Exception Plan covers the time period from the present moment to the end of the current stage and permits the Project Manager to show the change in work required to meet the new situation, the costs and the new tolerances set by the Project Board.

Product-based Planning

PRINCE uses a product-based planning technique. The reason for this is two-fold. The products have to be identified in order to consider what activities are needed in order to produce those products. The quality of a product can be measured and therefore planned for. The quality of an activity can only be measured by the quality of its outcome (the product).

The product-based planning technique is used by the process PL2, 'Define and Analyse the Products' in the common 'Planning' process.

Product-based planning has three components:

- Product Breakdown Structure
- Product Descriptions
- Product Flow Diagram.

PRODUCT BREAKDOWN STRUCTURE

Most planning methods begin a plan by thinking of the activities, and listing these in a hierarchical structure called a Work Breakdown Structure (WBS). PRINCE believes that the activities depend on what products are required to be produced by the project, and that the correct start point for a plan is to list the products.

A Product Breakdown Structure is a hierarchy of the products required to be produced by the plan. At the top is the final end-product, e.g. a system, a new yacht, a department relocated to a new building. This is then broken down into its major constituents at the next level. Each constituent is then broken down into its parts, and this process continues until the planner has reached the level of detail required for the plan.

Another important departure from other methods is the PRINCE emphasis that, apart from the Technical products of a project, there are always Management and Quality products. Listing these will remind us that they too take effort to produce and need to be planned as much as the production of Technical Products.

PRODUCT DESCRIPTION

For each identified product, at all levels of the Product Breakdown Structure, a description is produced. Its creation forces the planner to consider if sufficient is known about the product in order to plan its production. It is also the first time that the quality of the product is considered. The Quality Criteria indicate how much and what type of quality checking will be required.

The purposes of this are, therefore, to provide a guide:

- To the planner in how much effort will be required to create the product
- To the author of the product on what is required
- Against which the finished product can be measured.

These descriptions are a vital checklist to be used at a quality check of the related products.

The description should contain:

- The purpose of the product
- The products from which it is derived
- The composition of the product
- Any standards for format and presentation
- The quality criteria to be applied to the product
- The quality verification method to be used.

The Product Description is given to both the product's creator and those who will verify its quality.

PRODUCT FLOW DIAGRAM

The Product Flow Diagram is a diagram showing how a product is derived from another product or group of products.

Product-based Planning Example

A simple example is given in order to explain the PRINCE product-based planning technique. Please note – the example project is a very simple one, chosen so that the reader can concentrate on understanding the technique. What follows are the product-based planning steps for a small company which has decided to create a Christmas card containing a photograph and greeting from all the staff and send one to all its clients. They are going to do as much of the work themselves as is possible. The final output from this technique would feed into the remainder of the planning steps described in the 'Planning' (PL) process.

PRODUCT BREAKDOWN STRUCTURE EXAMPLE

With our example the final product will be 'Mailed Personal Christmas Cards'. We shall resist the temptation to say just 'Christmas cards' because the project won't be finished until the cards have been dispatched. The title reminds us of some extra work after the cards are ready.

Thinking of the Technical Products, our final product consists of:

- Fully prepared Christmas cards
- Envelopes
- Stamps.

We can now add to this list by working back in time and asking ourselves of each product, 'What product(s) do we need in order to build this?' For example, the envelopes won't be much good unless they have a name and address on them, the card needs designing. Our list of Technical Products might end up looking like Figure 5-2.

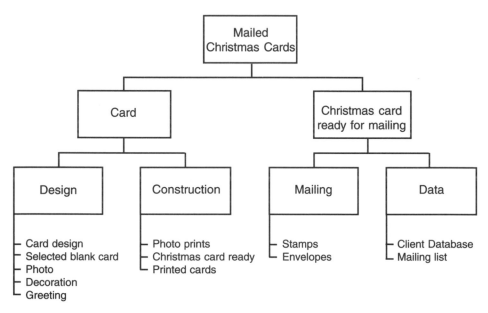

Figure 5-2. Product Breakdown Structure Example

The structure is an evolving one. Over the next steps, extra products may suggest themselves and be added to the structure.

MANAGEMENT AND QUALITY PRODUCTS

Having thought of the technical products, management and quality products should be listed. Management products include any contracts, all plans, control documents, progress reports, meeting minutes and approvals. An important management control at the beginning of every project is Project Initiation, where it is checked that justification of the project exists and everyone knows their responsibilities. Quality products include all the quality checking documents and Product Descriptions.

For this example the Management and Quality Products might look like those in Figure 5-3. PRINCE offers a general list of these products which can be used unchanged for most projects.

Management Products	**Quality Products**
Terms of Reference	Product Descriptions
Plans	Quality Review Documents
Plan Approvals	Quality Plans
Reports	Change Control Documents
Project Initiation Documents	

Figure 5-3. Management and Quality Products Example

CREATE PRODUCT DESCRIPTIONS

A Product Description for the staff Christmas photograph in the example would look like:

Title

Staff Christmas Photograph

Purpose

- To be the original from which copies can be taken for the company Christmas card

- To remind clients of the company name and services offered

- To help create a feeling of a more personal relationship between clients and members of staff

- To link the company and staff with the sentiments of well-being, friendliness and family in the eyes of clients.

Composition
- All staff
- Company logo (either building, company van or overalls)
- Yuletide trappings.

Derivation
- Staff list
- Professional quality camera and film
- A dozen poses
- Professional film development.

Quality Criteria
- Sharp, clear photo of everyone and company logo
- Prominent position of company logo
- Everyone in clean, smart attire representative of their work
- Everyone looking happy and waving at camera
- Gives a general Yuletide feeling.

Quality Verification Method
- Trial photos of proposed logo, Yuletide trappings and lighting to be used to be checked out before assembling staff
- Final choice – Managing Director to select from one dozen poses.

PRODUCT FLOW DIAGRAM EXAMPLE

Time flows in one direction only. The diagram begins with the Technical Products, and considers what is available at the start of the project and ends with the required final products (deliverables). Any products which are expected to be already available or coming from outside sources are shown in an ellipse. All products to be created by the project are shown in boxes. The derivation of a product is shown by drawing an arrow to it from each of the products from which it is derived.

In tracing the product flow in this way, extra interim products may be identified which are required to build and support the final products.

Products which exist outside the project and are needed in the building of the new products will also be discovered. For example, a Feasibility Study for it may have already been done as part of the overall strategy work, or a description of the current product may already exist. Any extra products discovered in this way are added to the Product Breakdown Structure.

After putting all the technical products into the Product Flow Diagram, the management and quality products are examined to see if they should be brought into the flow. Products such as plans, contracts and quality reviews should be added to the diagram. The previous comment about discovering extra products also applies to those needed to ensure the quality and management of the project, such as test and implementation strategies.

Figure 5-4 is a Product Flow Diagram for the Christmas card project.

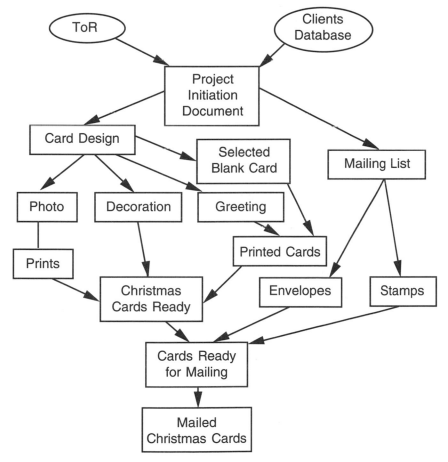

Figure 5-4. Product Flow Diagram Example

Plan Contents

A plan does not consist of only a Bar Chart or a Gantt Chart. This is simply a pictorial representation of resources working on products over a time period.

The contents of a plan are:

- The products to be produced
- The approach to be taken, the standards to be used
- The activities to produce (and quality check) those products
- The responsibilities and the resources needed to carry out those activities
- The internal and external dependencies
- The time frame of the activities
- The cost of the plan
- The prerequisites
- The assumptions on which the plan is based
- The risks involved in the plan
- The tolerance margins to be used
- The controls to be applied
- The reports to be produced.

6 | Project Controls

Why are Controls Needed?

It cannot be assumed that everything will go according to plan. There is a need to check progress against plan and be prepared to modify the plan in the light of events.

The Project Board has a responsibility to senior management to ensure that money is being well spent and that the solution produced will meet the stated business need. The Project Manager is responsible to the Project Board for the production of the required products within the agreed time, budget and quality constraints. Team managers are responsible to the Project Manager for the delivery of authorised Work Packages. Team members provide the products agreed with their Team Managers.

At each level there are expectations of the level below and a need to be informed if those expectations are not going to be met. There is also a need for regular assurance that the expectations will be met.

Overview of Project Controls

The above reasons mean that reports are needed from one level to the next. And in the case of things going wrong, each project needs to decide at what point the alarm bells should ring. If things do go wrong, what action should be taken, and at what level?

Project control consists of three iterative elements: planning, monitoring and controlling. The plan plots what should be done, by whom and estimates how long it will take. Monitoring checks on what actually happens. Control acts on the monitoring information and decides if the plan needs to be modified. To make an analogy with a ship, planning charts the course across the ocean, monitoring checks the real position against the

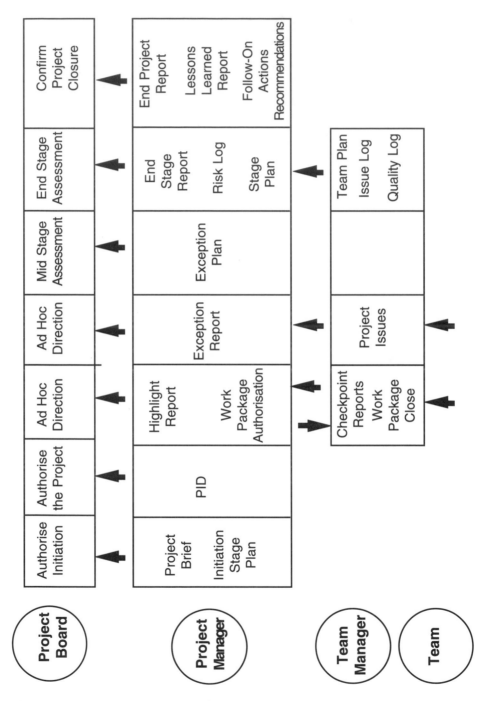

Figure 6-1. Overview of Project Controls

plotted course, and controlling adjusts the bearing and speed to compensate for any deviation caused by wind and currents.

A major element of control is reporting, which inputs information to the monitoring process. Figure 6-1 shows the reporting between the levels.

Project Board Controls

STARTING UP A PROJECT

Senior management control the inception of a project by the issue of the Project Mandate, appointment of the Project Board Executive and Project Manager.

THE PROJECT INITIATION MEETING

At the end of the process 'Start Up the Project', (SU), the Project Board controls further work by approving three management products, the Project Brief, the Project Management Team appointments and the Initiation Stage Plan.

The Project Brief

This defines the objectives of the project and therefore gives the Project Board the opportunity at the outset to ensure that the project is headed in the right direction. The brief often includes an outline business case, allowing the Project Board to confirm at an early stage that there is reasonable justification for expenditure on the project.

Project Management Team Appointments

By matching these against the Project Brief, the correct representations can be checked.

Initiation Stage Plan

This enables the Project Board to check the resources requested to expand the project definition, confirm the business case and plan the project. If it is not happy with the plan, the Project Board can insist on its revision or cancel the project.

Authorise the Project

At the end of initiation the Project Board looks at two documents before deciding whether to approve the next stage.

The Project Initiation Document

This document contains such information as the project definition, the initial project plan, the number and timing of project stages, the business case, a review of the risks facing the project. If the Project Board does not like what it reads, it may cancel or revise the project.

The Next Stage Plan

The Project Board has three sets of facts to examine before it gives approval to continue: the information in the Project Initiation Document, how well the Project Manager fared against the Initiation Stage Plan and the Next Stage Plan.

Tolerance

Tolerances are established to say when alarm bells should ring. They should be established by senior management for the whole project and apportioned out for each stage by the Project Board. The idea behind tolerances is that no project ever meets 100 percent of a plan. Should the Project Board worry if at one time a stage seems one day behind schedule or £10 under budget? If the answer is 'no', then the next question for the Project Board is 'how far wide of the plan should we allow things to deviate before we take action?' The answer to this question sets the tolerance levels.

Tolerances should cover at least time and budget. They are often expressed as a percentage. For example, on a total budget of £100,000 a 5 percent tolerance would mean that the project could come in anywhere within the range of £105,000 to £95,000 without alarming the Project Board. Tolerances need not be expressed as percentages. They may be expressed in terms of money or a number of days.

It may not be the same percentage for time and budget. There is no reason why they should not differ. For example, a fixed deadline may mean no time tolerance can be given. How can the Project Manager react to this? It should mean a larger budget tolerance, allowing the Project Manager to use extra resources, overtime or better resources in order to meet the fixed deadline. And vice versa. With zero tolerance on the budget, the Project Manager should argue for a greater time tolerance, allowing the use of fewer resources, the early release of resources or the use of cheaper (and probably less skilled) resources.

What if no tolerance is given on both time and budget? The third 'tolerance' option available to the Project Manager is to de-scope the product, i.e. if the project gets into trouble with either time or budget (or both), the Project Manager has a prioritised list of the customer's requirements and drops off items from the bottom of this list until left with elements which the project can deliver within the tolerances.

Watch out for an unofficial fourth option. When they feel under pressure to deliver, the team may reduce the amount of quality checking in order to fit within the tolerances.

END STAGE ASSESSMENT

Part of the PRINCE philosophy has always been the concept of 'creeping commitment'. This means that, as part of its control, the Project Board only commits to the next stage of the project. At the end of that stage, the situation is reviewed and the next stage is authorised only if the Project Board is satisfied with progress.

At the end of each stage the Project Manager has to present to the Project Board:

- How well the stage fared against the approved plan
- What impact the actual results have had on the Project Plan
- The plan for the next stage
- What impact this plan will have on the Project Plan and the Business Case
- A review of the risks facing the project.

The Project Board has full control at this time and can decide to stop, continue, ask for a plan revision or change the scope of the project.

Highlight Reports

Between End Stage Assessments the Project Manager gives a Highlight Report to the Project Board, assessing progress and real or potential problems, and forecasting progress over the next period. The Project Board decide on the frequency of these reports at project initiation time and the precise content. It is sensible that there is a standard for the content across a site or company, so that new Project Board members know what to expect. With small projects the Project Board may decide that the Highlight Reports may be given verbally rather than in writing.

Product Checklist

The Product Checklist is output from the stage planning process. It lists the major products of the stage with their expected dates of appearing in draft, quality checked and approved forms. As the stage progresses, the actual dates are filled in. The Product Checklist often accompanies the Highlight Report to give the Project Board a summary of the current status of the stage products.

Exception Reports

If the Project Manager forecasts that tolerances are going to be exceeded, an Exception Report must be given to the Project Board. A full description of the suggested contents of this is given in the Appendix 'Product Descriptions'. It is an early warning to the Project Board, describing the anticipated deviation and its impact, listing alternatives and making a recommendation. The Project Board's normal reaction will be to ask the Project Manager to produce an Exception Plan for presentation to the Board at a Mid Stage Assessment.

Exception Plan

An Exception Plan covers the period from the present time to the end of the current stage. It has the same format as the Stage Plan and contains the remaining work of the stage modified to include the work to react to the situation described in the Exception Report.

Mid Stage Assessment

These are unplanned meetings where an Exception Plan is presented to the Project Board for its approval.

So the control process is:

- The Project Board set tolerance controls for a stage
- The Project Manager has to inform the Project Board of any potential deviation beyond those tolerances
- The Project Board makes a decision on what to do
- The Project Manager produces a new plan to implement that decision
- The new plan only lasts until the stage end, when the normal end stage controls come into play.

The format of the meeting is very similar to an End Stage Assessment, except that the old Stage Plan will not have been completed.

Closing the Project

The Project Board can close the project at any time if it decides that the Business Case cannot be met or the risks are too great. If the project comes to a normal close, the Project Board still control this. It checks that all expected products have been delivered, that the customer is satisfied, and that the group to whom the end-product is being handed is ready and willing to accept responsibility. Any follow-on actions are passed to the appropriate group and a plan is confirmed to check on attainment of the project's Business Case.

Project Manager Controls

Work Package Authorisation

Part of the Project Manager's control is that no work is done until it is issued as an authorised Work Package (see the process 'Control the Stage' (CS1)). Product Descriptions of a Work Package and Work Package Authorisation are given in the Appendix to this book.

The Work Package describes the job to be done, the standards to be used and how the quality is to be checked. The authorisation identifies the person or team allocated the work, notes the agreed time and effort for the job, and states how the completed work is to be approved and returned.

A Work Package can be as big or as small as the Project Manager wishes, depending on the closeness of control to be exercised.

PROGRESS FEEDBACK

The Project Manager arranges for feedback on progress against the Stage Plan. The feedback may be in the form of timesheets or any other means to indicate actual progress and effort spent against the plan. This allows the Project Manager to monitor where the stage is compared to where it was planned to be, and adjust the plan if necessary.

CHECKPOINT REPORTS

The Project Manager also arranges for each Team Manager to feed back progress details via Checkpoint Reports. The frequency of these is decided by the Project Manager, and is usually tied to the need to provide the Project Board with Highlight Reports. Such reports flesh out the bare details provided by plan updates and give the Team Manager an opportunity to record concerns, problems, what is to be achieved in the next period, or the need for new Work Packages.

Checkpoint meetings, which generate the reports can also be used to pass information down the chain of command.

ISSUE LOG

The Issue Log is the central register of all questions, change requests and reported difficulties in meeting customer requirements. If the Project Manager enforces the discipline of using this mechanism, regular inspection of the log will provide details of unexpected events which might affect the project. The Project Manager is in control of the Issue Log and gives first direction on the action to take about an issue. Together with checking progress against the Stage Plan and receiving Checkpoint Reports, this builds the Project Manager's control of what is happening in the stage.

RISK LOG

An important element of control is the control of risks to the project. PRINCE requires that the Project Manager analyses and evaluates risks as part of project initiation and at the end of each stage. These are the minimum number of times. In medium to large projects, the frequency may need to be greater.

The Risk Log not only identifies each risk but records the current status of each risk and who is looking after that risk. By understanding what is on the Risk Log, the Project Manager can watch progress feedback for anything which might affect the risks.

QUALITY LOG

The Quality Log records all the quality checks carried out in the project. Team Managers update the log when a quality check is done. By checking the Quality Log against the issued Work Packages, the Project Manager can monitor that the quality work is being done.

CONFIGURATION STATUS ACCOUNT

The Configuration Status Account gives the Project Manager information on the status of products, particularly those from the current stage. The Project Manager can compare this with the Stage Plan, progress feedback and Checkpoint Reports to ensure the correct information is being given.

CONFIGURATION AUDIT

As part of control, the Project Manager needs to be sure that the various products of the project are being controlled. The audit, usually carried out by one of the Project Assurance Team, checks that the 'paper' records match actual fact, i.e. if the current version of product x is 3, do the records show that, or do they think that version 2 is still the latest?

Team Manager Controls

WORK PACKAGE

Work Packages are agreed with the Project Manager. The agreement is a two-way control in that the Project Manager can ensure that the Stage Plan matches the time and effort figures agreed with the Team Manager, and the Team Manager can negotiate the figures to ensure the achievement of the work is a reasonable expectation. The Work Package Authorisation contains how the work is to be quality checked and by whom, and also details how the products are to be approved and returned.

Team Plan Review

On the basis of Work Package Authorisations the Team Manager prepares a plan for the team to carry out the work. Progress reviews against this plan give feedback to the Team Manager. Depending on the plan updates or information received at Checkpoint Meetings, the Team Manager may need to adjust the plan.

Checkpoint Meetings

In order to prepare Checkpoint Reports for the Project Manager, the Team Manager holds Checkpoint Meetings with the team. This gives an opportunity to hear of any problems at first hand, i.e. monitoring the situation, and react as necessary (the control part of the plan-monitor-control cycle).

7 | The Business Case

Why?

Before major expenditure on the project, its viability and worth should be considered. Why are we doing the project? Does everyone involved have the same vision of the reasons for the project? Is this a sensible way of spending scarce resources and budget? Are there other projects which would show a better return on the investment? Will the end product's useful life be long enough to recoup the investment and show a profit?

Where and When in PRINCE?

The Business Case is formalised during the Initiation Stage as part of the Project Board's information to be examined before deciding whether to go ahead with the project. There may have been an earlier Feasibility Study where a basic Business Case was developed in order to choose between alternative options. If so, this would be the basis of the project's Business Case, refined during Initiation.

Far too often the Business Case is prepared just for the Project Initiation Document and/or to obtain the funds and then forgotten. It should be revised as the project situation develops, reacting to the actual costs and times from a stage, the detailed planning figures for a new stage and to any external changes.

Minimally the Business Case should be updated as part of the preparation for each End Stage Assessment. It is a major source of data for the Project Board when it is considering whether to continue with the project and approve the next Stage Plan. If an Exception Plan has to be raised, the Business Case is a key input again to the Project Board decision.

Who?

The Project Board Executive is accountable for the existence of a viable Business Case. The Project Manager is responsible for its production.

If the Executive has delegated the role's assurance responsibilities, the Business Assurance Co-ordinator monitors any changes to the scenario pictured in the Business Case throughout the project. This includes examining change requests for their impact on the Business Case.

What Should the Business Case Contain?

REASONS

The reasons for undertaking a project should be documented. Examples of reasons include:

- Legislation
- Legal requirements
- Company policy
- The old age of the current product
- The inability of the current product to meet new requirements
- A lack of capacity in the current product
- A better, faster, cheaper, more accurate way of doing a job
- A new requirement which hasn't been encountered before
- Technology has made it possible to do a job which couldn't be done before
- The end of an existing contract
- Keeping up with competition
- Needed to support the aims of a parent programme.

INVESTMENT APPRAISAL

This is a comparison of the costs of developing, operating and maintaining the product against the benefits and savings expected from the product's use.

An important point, often overlooked, is to ensure that the basis used to measure each item in the Investment Appraisal (before the event) is the same basis as can be used to measure the actual costs and benefits after the event. Too often figures are quoted in the Business Case in order to obtain funds which prove impossible to quantify after the product is in use. Figure 7-1 provides a focus for an explanation of this.

	0	1	2	3	4	5	CHECKED BY
Benefits							at Initiation by PB/PM
and Savings							
xxxxxxxx							Post implementation by ?
xxxxxxxx							
Project costs							
xxxxxxxx							
Operational and							At initiation by PB/PM
maintenance costs							
xxxxxxxx							Post implementation by ?
xxxxxxxx							
Discounted							
cash flow							

Figure 7-1. The example covers a project which takes two years to deliver the product (years 0 and 1)

PROJECT COST

This is a calculation of the development costs of the product and the time frame over which those costs are accrued. These costs are normally straightforward to identify and calculate, but care must be taken to look at every aspect. For example, will there be any conversion costs, including re-training user staff?

OPERATIONAL COST

This is a calculation per year of the costs of operating and maintaining the product.

The Post Implementation Review will be held some time in year 2 in the example above. It is important to consult the operational support staff when identifying the costs and the ways in which these costs are measured. For example, there is no point in putting in a figure for fair wear and tear unless there is (or you can agree with the operations staff) an accepted method of calculating this.

Examples of operational costs are:

- Operational staff
- Rental and royalty charges
- Consumables
- Equipment use
- Raw materials.

The other half of operational cost is the cost of maintenance. This is again a tricky area. Are we speaking strictly of maintenance (correcting faults, strengthening elements, value engineering, but basically meeting the original requirement) or are we also talking about enhancement of the product to do things which were not part of the original specification? The latter should be part of the Business Case of the enhancement projects, but are we set up to differentiate between the two types of cost? If not, can we establish this division of costs so that the original Business Case figures can be genuinely compared with results?

As Figure 7-1 shows, the Business Case does not stop after one year, but covers, typically three to five years. The Post Implementation Review will be held much earlier than this. The Investment Appraisal must show a forecast of the operational costs at the time of the Post Implementation Review as well as for the whole length of the Investment Appraisal.

BENEFITS AND SAVINGS

This is an estimate of the monetary value of the benefits and savings to be gained by using the product. It is important that the estimates come from those who will use the product or gain from its use, i.e. those represented by the Senior User and Executive roles.

It is important that benefits and savings are stated in measurable terms wherever possible. Terms such as 'better, faster, cheaper' should be avoided. How much faster? Five percent? Ten percent? Is there an accurate figure for the current time taken? What will be measured in order to work out the percentage gain? What costs will be taken into account when working out the cheapness? How will any improvement be measured? Rather than say 'We want the new payroll system to be cheaper to run' it is better to say 'The new system must cost no more than one penny per payslip produced'.

Many users will look only for the benefits of the new product and forget the costs of not having the new product. For example, if it is a replacement product, there are operational and maintenance costs associated with the current product which will be saved when the new product is brought in. Might there be any penalty payments caused by not having the new product? For example, 'To meet government legislation' may seem to be a reason which cannot be quantified. But if the product does not meet legislation, then perhaps:

- The legislative requirements have to be met by manual procedures which have a cost

- The current product cannot continue to be used, losing the current revenue or savings it brings

- There will be penalties imposed by the government

- The company may be exposed to expensive court cases brought by customers.

The same point is made here as was made for the costs. When can the benefits be measured? The implicit assumption is that there can be some measurement at Post Implementation Review time. Will all benefits be clear by this time? If the Investment Appraisal covers five years, will the benefits continue to be measured over this period of time? Will it be possible after five years to check the effectiveness of the product against its Business Case?

GAP ANALYSIS

Here GAP stands for 'Good – Average – Poor'.

Benefits and savings are usually estimates rather than hard fact. In such cases, it is useful to assess whether the estimates are optimistic, pessimistic or somewhere in the middle. Three Investment Appraisals can thus be done where the Business Case for the project may be tenuous. One appraisal takes a 'good' view of the benefits, one takes a 'poor' view, and the third is the 'average' or most likely estimate.

DISCOUNTED CASH FLOW

The idea behind this concept is that there is a difference in the value of money today and the value of that same money in one, two years time. As an example, a house costing £5,000 in 1970 would have looked quite expensive in most parts of the UK. A house for £5,000 in 1996 would be unbelievably cheap. Inflation tends to reduce the value of our money, so to find out the value of a product in five years time we have to apply a discount factor. Over the past few years the standard discount figure has been 6 percent. In a sense, it is like asking the questions:

- how much will we get back over five years if we invest this amount in product development today?

- How much will we get back over five years if we invest this amount with a bank or building society?

The first option carries far more risk, so the expected return should include a premium for taking that risk.

ASSUMPTIONS

The Business Case should be scrutinised for any assumptions and these carefully documented. There may be assumptions, for example, on:

- inflation

- each benefit and saving

- the development schedule

- the economic life of the end product

- the residual value of the product at the end of its useful life.

The important ones here are the assumptions about each benefit and saving. Very often they require management to make decisions in order to achieve the expectation. There may be staff performance levels involved in achieving the savings or benefits, so matters such as motivation come into the equation which are beyond the remit of most projects. (Some projects do, however, include such end products as 'trained and motivated staff' and allow for the costs of achieving these products.)

Forms

Below are two forms which will provide a start for the design of forms suitable to develop the necessary figures for an Investment Appraisal. The Operational Costs form can be used for both the new and the current product by ticking the appropriate box.

The forms are set out for a computer project, but they will trigger the relevant headings for any other type of project.

OPERATIONAL COSTS							
Project					Date		
Current product				New product			
	Yr 0	Yr 1	Yr 2	Yr 3	Yr 4	Yr 5	Total
Hardware							
Rental or purchase							
Maintenance							
Network							
Software							
Rental or purchase							
Maintenance							
Manpower							
User departments							
IT department							
Operations							
Other							
Administration							
Overheads							
Materials							
Stationery							
Consumables							
Total Operating Cost							

Figure 7-2. Operational Costs Form.

COST/BENEFIT ANALYSIS							
Project Date							
	Yr 0	Yr 1	Yr 2	Yr 3	Yr 4	Yr 5	Total
Costs							
Development							
Resources							
Other costs							
Running costs							
Total costs							
Savings							
Current system							
Benefits							
Total benefits							
Cash flow							
Discounted cash flow							

Figure 7-3. Cost/Benefit Analysis Form

8 | Management of Risk

Risk can be formally defined as:

'The chance of exposure to the adverse consequences of future events.'

In a project, risk is anything which causes the project to end in such a way that it does not fully meet its identified targets and objectives.

The management of risk is one of the most important parts of the Project Board's and Project Manager's jobs. The effect of failure to deliver a project on time, to an acceptable cost and level of quality can be disastrous. Although the cost of managing risk may appear significant, the cost of not managing risk effectively can be many times greater. The Project Manager has the responsibility to ensure that risks are identified, recorded and regularly reviewed. The Project Board has two responsibilities:

- To notify the Project Manager of any external risk exposure to the project
- To make decisions on the Project Manager's recommended reactions to risk.

In a customer/supplier environment, each party may have a different set of risks to which they feel exposed, or will have a different view of a risk and the alternative actions. The customer will try to protect the achievement of its business case and get the supplier to take the risks (or bear the cost of any preventive or avoiding action). The supplier will try to protect the expected profit margin and therefore take the opposite view. The customer's project manager (or project authority by another name) is responsible for ensuring that the appropriate level of information is gathered from all sources to enable a true assessment of risk to be made.

The key decisions on risk management are made by the Project Board, and an important benefit of PRINCE is that the Project Board represents all the parties; the customer, the user and the supplier.

Addressing Risk

Only by fully recognising and understanding the risks which exist can potential problems and opportunities be understood and addressed. Both the likelihood of things happening and the consequences if they do occur must be understood by the project management team in order to have this true appreciation of the risk situation. The Project Board then needs to choose a course of action which can be taken to improve the situation.

It should be recognised that it may be desirable to accept some risks in order to obtain additional benefits to the project. *Note*: the option to take no action may sometimes be appropriate. This means that a decision is made that the perceived level of risk is acceptable.

How effectively a risk can be managed depends on the identification of its underlying causes and the amount of control that the project management team can exert over these. It is more effective to reduce the potential cause of a risk than to wait for that risk to materialise and then address its impact.

The impact of a risk which materialises should not be mistaken for the underlying cause of the risk. For example, *cost escalation* on a project is an ever-present risk impact. Expenditure should be monitored to determine the underlying causes of risk, that is *why* costs are escalating.

Continuous Monitoring and Management of Risk

It is important that the management of risk is considered as a continuous process throughout the life of a project. Once potential risks have been identified they need to be monitored until such time as either they cease to be material, or their effect has been reduced or mitigated as a result of management intervention. The potential for new risks being introduced with time, or in consequence of actions taken, also needs to be considered throughout the project life-cycle. The obvious times for risk assessment and management are:

- Project initiation
- End stage assessment

and these should be considered the minimum number of times. Depending on the project's criticality and size, risks should be examined regularly, say, each month.

Responsibilities

In broad terms, the Project Manager is responsible for seeing that risk analysis is done, the Project Board responsible for the management of risk (the decisions on courses of action to take). In practice the Project Manager may take decisions on certain risks where the consequences are within the tolerance margins, but even there it would be wise to advise the Project Board in the Highlight Report of any such decisions.

It is good practice to appoint one individual as responsible for monitoring each identified risk, the person best placed to observe the factors which affect that risk. According to the risk, this may be a member of the Project Board, someone with assurance duties, the Project Manager, Team Manager or a team member.

An Approach to the Management of Risk

PRINCE uses a Risk Log to record and keep track of each identified risk. A Product Description of a Risk Log is provided in the Appendix to this book.

PRINCE does not insist on a particular method of risk management. There are many possible methods, techniques or software tools which will assist in the management of risk. PRINCE gives a general description of an approach which is compatible with the one recommended by the CCTA. This, in turn, is in line with RISKMAN, the European Project Risk Management Methodology.

Figure 8-1 is a summary of such an approach.

Although the management of risk is a cyclic process, it can be considered to have two main parts, risk analysis (the gathering of information about risks and the preparation of alternatives) and risk management (decision-making, taking action and watching what happens). These two parts are divided into the seven major activities shown in Figure 8-1.

Risk Analysis

Risk analysis comprises three overlapping activities, whose purpose is shown in the following table.

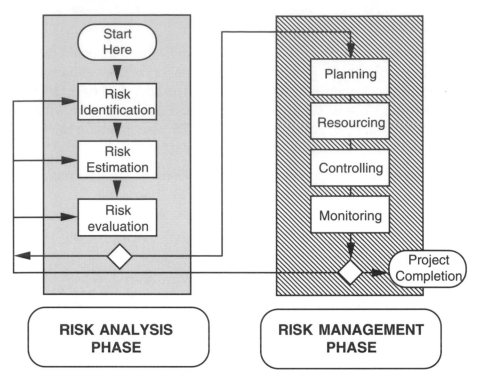

Figure 8-1. The major activities in the management of risk

ACTIVITY	PURPOSE
Risk identification	Preparing a list of all the potential risks which could be faced by the project
Risk estimation	Determining how important each risk is, based upon an assessment of its likelihood and consequences to the project and the business
Risk evaluation	Deciding whether the level of each risk is acceptable or not and, if not, what actions can be taken to make it more acceptable.

RISK IDENTIFICATION

It is important to list all possible risks, not to mentally exclude any because it is instinctively felt that 'it will not happen' or 'that would not be serious'. That is the purpose of the second activity, which cannot be done for any risk which is not listed. What one person feels to be unlikely may appear to be very likely to someone else who has different information about it.

RISK ESTIMATION

In determining the likelihood and impact of a risk, a simple method is to award each risk one of three categories, High, Medium or Low. This would provide sufficient information for the third activity for most projects. Looking at a sample matrix for a risk shown in Figure 8-2:

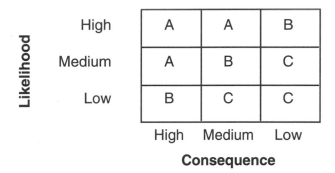

Likelihood	High	A	A	B
	Medium	A	B	C
	Low	B	C	C
		High	Medium	Low

Consequence

Figure 8-2. Risk matrix

If a risk is estimated to fall into one of the squares marked 'A', it would represent a major risk. Risks with a category of 'B' would represent intermediate risks, and category 'C' risks would be minor risks.

RISK EVALUATION

Risk evaluation covers:

- Assessing the acceptable level of each risk
- Generating alternative paths of action for risks which do not meet acceptability criteria
- Sorting the risks into a final order of priority
- Cross-referencing them to the identified risk reduction options.

This step takes the estimates from the previous step and has to balance the cost of counter-measures against the cost of allowing the risk to occur. This is where it is useful to have graded risks as, for example, major, intermediate and minor. Major risks would require action (risk avoidance if possible) before proceeding. Intermediate risks might need counter-measures, but there would be a more careful eye on the cost of these. In many cases the decision might be to have a contingency plan to implement if the risk occurs, i.e. spend very little money ahead of the need. Minor risks are likely to be the ones accepted.

All risks need to be monitored, their seriousness dictating the frequency of monitoring. As stated earlier, monitoring should be allocated to an individual for each risk.

There is a standard list of categories of alternative actions, in the following order of preference:

- Eliminate the cause of the risk
- Reduce the likelihood of the risk occurring
- Reduce the direct consequences of the risk:
  - By a containment action
  - By a contingency plan
- Mitigate the ultimate consequences to the business:
  - By a containment action
  - By a contingency plan
- Transfer the risk to someone else (e.g. insurance)
- Gather more information before making a decision
- Accept the risk as it is.

Containment actions are normally preferable to contingency actions, but both can be used in the case of serious risks. Some examples of these two categories are:

- Containment
  - Employ people with better or different skills
  - Provide appropriate training
  - Reduce the product's functionality
  - Test the product more thoroughly.
- Contingent
  - Identify a second supplier
  - Identify other fall-back resources
  - Identify a fall-back plan
  - Establish a formal escalation process

Risk Management

Risk management consists of four major activities:

ACTIVITY	PURPOSE
Planning	Selecting the option most appropriate for each risk; developing a detailed plan of action; confirming its desirability and objectives; and obtaining management approval. This activity may proceed in parallel with risk evaluation
Resourcing	Identifying and assigning the resources necessary to do the work (including monitoring); confirming that the revised plan is feasible and cost-effective; checking the revised plan against the project Business Case
Monitoring	Checking the status of risks; checking that counter-measures are happening and are effective; capturing lessons learned on the effectiveness of risk reduction measures
Controlling	Making sure that execution of the plan is having the desired effect on the risks; ensuring that the management of risk processes are applied effectively; modifying the plan where necessary

PLANNING

The first question here is:

Do I need to do anything about this risk?

The answer will be based on the information from the analysis activities.

Choosing the best course of action is also part of this activity followed by revising the original plan to accommodate the counter-measures and monitoring activities.

The suggestion in the CCTA Management of Risk method is that the revised plan is then presented to the Project Board for approval. In practice, the Project Manager would be sensible to discuss the whole risk planning question with the Project Board informally and get its input to the selection of alternatives. Then the plan presentation would contain no surprises and should be quickly approved.

RESOURCING

Responsibilities, including monitoring, are allocated. After allocation, the plan should be checked to ensure that the resource allocation has not itself brought up any problems. After any necessary revision, the plan is put into operation.

MONITORING

All risks and their counter-measures should be regularly checked. For a medium project it may be sufficient to do this at each stage end. Large projects should also be done then, but also on, say, a monthly basis. Serious risks may need to be checked more frequently than this. Small projects with few stages are best suited to risk status checking at a frequency appropriate to the overall project duration. The activity includes any agreed reporting between those monitoring risks, the Project Manager and the Project Board.

CONTROLLING

This covers co-ordination of the risk management activities, ensuring that progress against the plan is within the resource limits, and modifying the plan in the light of events.

Illustrative List of Risk Analysis Questions

This section contains an illustrative list of questions which a project manager may require to have answered for a particular project. It is based on the CCTA publication, 'Management of Project Risk'.

BUSINESS/STRATEGIC

1. Do the project objectives fit into the organisation's overall business strategy?
2. When is the project due to deliver; how was the date determined?
3. What would be the result of late delivery?
4. What would be the result of limited success (functionality)?
5. What is the stability of the business area?

EXTERNAL FACTORS

1. Is this project exposed to requirements due to international interests? (i.e. are there legal implications from overseas, or are foreign companies involved)

2. Could there be 'political' implications of the project failing?

3. Is this project part of a programme? If so, what constraints are set for the project by that programme?

PROCUREMENT

1. Has the supplier a reputation for delivery of high quality goods?

2. Is the contract sufficiently detailed to show what the supplier is going to provide?

3. Are the acceptance criteria clear to both parties?

4. Is the contract legally binding/enforceable? (consideration should be given to topics including ownership rights and liability)

ORGANISATIONAL FACTORS

1. What consideration needs to be given to security for this project?

2. Does the project have wholehearted support from senior management?

3. What is the commitment of the user management?

4. Have training requirements been identified? Can these requirements be met?

MANAGEMENT

1. How clearly are the project objectives defined?

2. Will the project be run using a well-documented approach to project management?

3. Does this approach cover aspects of quality management, risk management and development activities in sufficient depth?

4. How well do the project team understand the chosen methodology?

5. What is the current state of project plans?

6. Is completion of this project dependent on the completion of others?

7. Are the tasks in the project plan inter-dependent? (and can the critical path through tasks be identified?)

8. What is the availability of appropriate resources? (What are the skills and experience of the project team? What is the make-up of the project team?)

9. Will people be available for training? (for IS projects this includes the project team, users and operations staff)

10. How many separate user functions are involved?

11. How much change will there be to the users operation or organisation?

TECHNICAL

1. Is the specification clear, concise, accurate and feasible?

2. How have the technical options been evaluated?

3. What is the knowledge of the equipment? (for IT, for example, this is the hardware/software environment)

4. Does the experience of the project manager cover a similar application?

5. Is this a new application?

6. What is the complexity of the system?

7. How many sites will the system be implemented in?

8. Is the proposed equipment new/leading edge? Is the proposed hardware/software environment in use already?

9. Who is responsible for defining system testing?

10. Who is responsible for defining acceptance testing?

11. On what basis is the implementation planned?

12. What access will the project team have to the development facilities?

13. Will the system be operated by the user or specialist staff?

14. Have requirements for long-term operations, maintenance and support been identified?

9 | Quality

The approach in PRINCE 2 to the provision of quality products is illustrated in Figure 9-1.

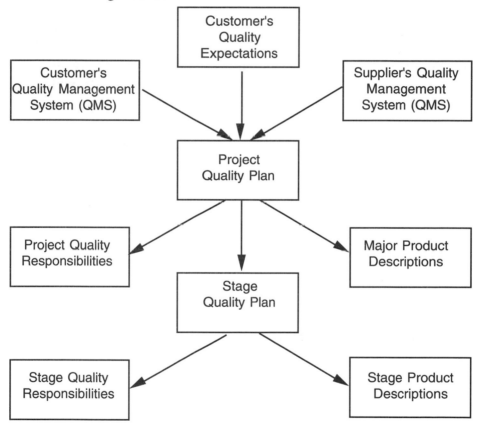

Figure 9-1. The PRINCE 2 Approach to Quality

The Customer's Quality Expectations

The customer's quality expectations should be made clear in the Project Mandate at the very outset of the project. If not sufficiently clear, the Project Manager should clarify the expectations when preparing the Project Brief (during 'Start Up the Project' (SU)). The expectations should be measurable. 'Of good quality' may sound fine, but how can it be measured? Expectations of performance, reliability, flexibility, maintainability, capability can all be expressed in measurable terms.

It is a mistake to believe that every product must be of top quality in every respect. Not every product is required to be beautifully polished, easy-to-use and capable of working for ever. There are products which are designed to be thrown away after one use, other products where early availability of the product is far more important than ease-of-use, flexibility or maintainability.

Quality is one corner of a triangle as shown in Figure 9-2. The customer has to decide where, within the triangle, the project's main focus is to be. Does it incline more towards the cost, the time or the quality? This simple exercise shows that the three items are inter-linked. If you want the product to be cheap, that may have an adverse effect on the quality, and so on.

Figure 9-2. The Quality, Cost and Time Triangle

The Project Quality Plan

The next step is to decide how the project is going to meet the customer's quality expectations for the product. Other inputs to this should be the standards to be used to guide the development of the product and test its ability to meet the quality expectations. The supplier should have standards, but the customer may also have standards which it insists on being used. Such standards have to be compared against the expectations to see which are to be used. There may be gaps where extra standards have to be obtained or created. The customer has the last say in what standards will be used to check the products.

The Project Quality Plan identifies the standards to be used and the main quality responsibilities. The latter may be a reference to a Quality Assurance function (belonging to either the customer, the supplier or both). There is a cross-reference here to the Project Board roles. These roles contain assurance responsibilities, some of them affecting quality. If these have been delegated, there must be a match with the responsibilities defined in the Project Quality Plan.

The Project Quality Plan refers to the establishment of the Quality Log, the Quality File and their purposes.

The plan also identifies the procedures which will be used to control changes and the Configuration Management Plan.

Product Descriptions are written for the key products shown in the Project Plan. These include specify quality criteria against which the products will be measured.

The Stage Quality Plan

Each stage has its own quality plan containing lower level detail than the Project Quality Plan. This identifies the method of quality checking to be used for each product of the stage.

The plan also identifies responsibilities for each individual quality check. For example, for each Quality Review the Chairman and Reviewers are identified. This gives an opportunity for the Project Assurance Team to see each draft Stage Plan and input its needs for checking and the staff who should represent it at each check.

Any major products developed in the stage have Product Descriptions written for them, if they were not done as part of the Project Quality Plan.

10 | Quality Review

What is a Quality Review?

This is a team method of assuring a document's quality by a review process. The purpose of the review is to inspect the product for errors in a planned, independent, controlled and documented manner and ensure that any errors found are fixed.

Why are Quality Reviews needed?

The major aim is to improve product quality. There are several subordinate objectives. These are to:

- Trap errors as early as possible

- Encourage the concept of products as team property rather than belonging to an individual

- Enhance product status data (i.e. not only has the creator declared it finished, but others have confirmed that it is of good quality)

- Monitor the use of standards

- Spread knowledge of the product among those whose own products may interact with it.

Quality Review documentation, when filed in the Quality File, provides with the Quality Log a record that the product was inspected, that any errors found were corrected and that the corrections were themselves checked. Knowing that a product has been checked and declared error-free provides a more confident basis to move ahead and use that product as the basis of future work.

People Involved

The **interests** of parties who should be considered when drawing up the list of attendees are:

- the product author (in PRINCE called the Producer)
- the Project Board
- those with assurance responsibilities delegated by the Project Board (the Project Assurance Team)
- the customer
- staff who will operate or maintain the finished product
- staff from other systems which will be affected by the product
- independent observers (perhaps to confirm the completeness of the procedures and the attitude of attendees)
- project management
- specialists in the relevant product area
- standards representatives.

Roles at the Quality Review

The **roles** involved in the Quality Review process are:

THE PRODUCER

This person is the author of the product being reviewed. This role has to ensure that the reviewers have all the required information in order to perform their job. This means getting a copy of the product to them during the preparation phase, plus any other documents needed to put it in context, then answering questions about the product during the review until a decision can be reached on whether there is an error or not. Finally the Producer will do most, if not all, of the correcting work.

The Producer must not be allowed to be defensive about the product.

THE CHAIRMAN

In choosing the person for this role, consideration must be given to the attitude of the Producer if that person's manager is to be present. An open, objective attitude is needed. Required attributes are:

- to be a project member but not the product author
- to have technical knowledge of the product
- to have sufficient authority to control the review
- to have chairmanship experience.

The Chairman is responsible for ensuring that the Quality Review is properly organised and that it runs smoothly during all of its phases.

For the Preparation phase this includes checking that administrative procedures have been carried out and that the right people have been invited. This needs consultation with the Project Assurance Team and reference to the Stage Plan.

THE REVIEWERS

The people appointed to these roles must be competent to assess the product from their particular viewpoints.

It must be remembered that these are roles. They must all be present at a Quality Review, but a person may take on more than one role.

Phases

There are three distinct phases within the Quality Review procedure: Preparation; Review; Follow-Up.

PHASE 1 – PREPARATION

The objective of this phase is to examine the product under review and to create a list of questions (or possible errors) for the review.

The Chairman checks with the Producer that the product will be ready on time. If not, the Project Manager is advised. This will lead to an update of the Stage Plan. The Chairman ensures that the team of Reviewers is agreed, that they will all be available and that the venue has been arranged.

An invitation is sent out, giving the time and place for the review with copies of the product, the relevant Product Description and any checklist available. This should be done with sufficient time before the review that the Reviewers have time to examine the document and provide a Question List to the Producer.

Each Reviewer will study the product and supporting documents (including the Quality Criteria included in the Product Description), annotate the product, and complete a Quality Review Question List.

A copy of the Question Lists will, wherever possible, be sent to the Producer before the review. These should be reviewed by Producer and Chairman to allow the Chairman to set up an agenda, prioritise the questions and roughly allocate time to each point. To save time at the review, the Producer can acknowledge questions which identify agreed errors.

PHASE 2 – REVIEW

The objective of the review is to agree a list of any actions needed to correct or complete the product. The Chairman and the Producer do not have to reconcile these actions at the meeting – it is sufficient for the Chairman and Reviewers to agree that a particular area needs re-examination. Provided that the action is logged the Reviewers have an opportunity to confirm that action has been taken.

The Chairman opens the meeting and introduces those present if necessary. Timing (suggested maximum of 2 hours) is announced.

The Producer then 'walks through' the questions in detail. This will be determined by the Reviewers' Question Lists already sent to the Producer. If it is found that any part is understood and accepted, there is no point in walking through it.

The Chairman controls the discussion during the walk-through ensuring that no arguments or solutions are discussed (other than obvious and immediately accepted solutions!). Follow-Up actions are noted on a Follow-Up Action List by the Scribe. No minutes are taken of the review.

At the conclusion of the walk-through, the Chairman asks the Scribe to read back the Follow-Up actions and determines responsibility for correction of any points. A target date is set for each action and the initials of the

Reviewer(s) who will sign-off each corrective action as done and acceptable are recorded on the Follow-Up Action Sheet by the Scribe.

The Chairman, after seeking the Reviewers' and Producer's opinions, will decide on the outcome of the review. There can be one of three outcomes:

- The product is error-free

- The product will be acceptable on completion of the actions noted

- There is so much corrective work to be done that the entire product needs to be re-reviewed.

In the latter case, the Chairman will advise the Project Manager so that the Stage Plan can be updated. A result notification will be completed and the documents attached. These forms will be filed in the Quality File and the Quality Log updated.

The Reviewers' Question Lists, copies of the product (probably containing the Reviewer's annotations) and any other relevant documentation is collected by the Chairman and passed to the Producer to assist in the Follow-Up.

PHASE 3 – FOLLOW-UP

The objective of the Follow-Up phase is to ensure that all actions identified on the Follow-Up Action List are dealt with.

The Producer takes the list away from the review and evaluates, discusses, and corrects, if necessary, all the errors.

When an error has been fixed, the Producer will obtain sign-off from whoever is nominated on the Follow-Up Action List. This person may be the Reviewer who raised the query initially, but other Reviewers have the option of checking the correction.

When all errors have been reconciled and sign-off obtained, the Chairman will confirm that the product is complete and sign off the Follow-Up Action List. The documents will be filed in the Quality File, the Quality Log and the Stage Plan updated.

Quality Review Responsibilities

Chairman's responsibilities

Preparation

1. Check with the Producer that the product is ready for review.
2. If not, update the Stage Plan, e.g. a revised completion date.
3. Consult with the Producer and the Project Assurance Team to confirm appropriate Reviewers.
4. Agree the amount of preparation time required with the Reviewers.
5. Arrange a time, location and duration for the review in consultation with the Producer and Reviewers.
6. Advise the Project Manager if there is to be any delay in holding the review.
7. Arrange for copies of any relevant checklist or standard to be provided.
8. Ensure the Configuration Librarian provides Product Descriptions and product copies for all Reviewers.
9. Send an invitation, Product Description, product copy, checklist and standard to each Reviewer.
10. Send a copy of the invitation to the Producer.
11. Decide if a short overview presentation of the product to the reviewers is required prior to the review, and arrange it if it is.
12. Arrange with the Reviewers for collection of their Question Lists prior to the review.
13. Create an agenda for the review from the Question Lists in consultation with the Producer. Agree any obvious errors with the Producer. Prioritise the questions and roughly allocate time.
14. Confirm attendance with each Reviewer shortly before the review. If a Reviewer cannot attend, ensure that the Reviewer's Question List is made out and submitted. If too many Reviewers cannot attend, re-schedule the review and inform the Project Manager.
15. If necessary, rehearse the review with the Producer.

Review

1. Provide a copy of the agenda to all attendees.

2. Open the review, stating objectives and apologising for any non-attendees.

3. Decide whether the Reviewers present and the Question Lists from any unable to attend are adequate to review the product. If not, the review should be stopped, re-scheduled and the Project Manager advised.

4. Identify any errors already agreed by the Producer and ensure that these are documented on the Follow-Up Action List.

5. Step through the agenda, with the appropriate Reviewer enlarging where necessary on the question.

6. Allow reasonable discussion on each question between Producer and Reviewers to decide if action is required.

7. Document any agreed actions required on a Follow-Up Action List.

8. Prevent any discussion of possible solutions or matters of style.

9. Ensure every Reviewer is given a chance to voice their comments.

10. Where agreement cannot be reached on a point in a reasonable time frame, declare it an action point and note the Reviewer(s) concerned.

11. Where necessary, decide on the premature close of the review in the light of the comments made.

12. If faults are identified in products not under review, ensure that a Project Issue is raised and sent to the Configuration Librarian.

13. Collect any annotated products detailing minor or typographical errors.

14. Read back the Follow Up Action List and obtain confirmation from the Producer and Reviewers that it is complete and correct.

15. Identify who is to be involved in working on each action item. Obtain a target date for completion of the work.

16. Agree with the Reviewers who is to approve the work done on each action item and note this on the Follow-Up Action List.

17. Pass the Follow-Up Action List and all copies of the annotated product to the Producer. Lodge a copy of the Follow-Up Action List in the Quality File.

18. Decide with the Reviewers the status of the product. It can be:

    • Complete with no errors discovered

    • Complete with some re-work required

    • In need of re-work and another review.

19. If the review is incomplete, recommend a course of action to the Project Manager. There are five possible courses of action. The last two of these are not recommended:

    • The product should be re-worked prior to another review

    • The review should be reconvened to finish with no interim need for re-work

    • The review should be reconvened without re-work with a different set of reviewers

    • The review should be declared complete, the errors found so far corrected and the rest of the product accepted as is

    • The review should be abandoned and the product used as is, i.e. none of the errors corrected, but noted in a Project Issue.

Follow-Up

1. Monitor the correction of errors and sign off the Follow-Up Action List when all corrections have been approved.

2. If an action cannot be taken within the time allowed, the Chairman and Producer may decide to transfer it to a Project Issue as a possible Off-Specification. This requires the agreement of the Project Manager. The Follow-Up Action List is updated with the Project Issue log number and those waiting to sign off the action item informed.

3. On completion and sign-off of all action items, sign off the Follow-Up Action List as complete and file it in the Quality File with copies to all reviewers. Update the Quality Log.

4. Supervise the passage of the error-free product to the Configuration Librarian.

PRODUCER'S RESPONSIBILITIES

Preparation

1. Ask the Project Manager to nominate a Chairman if none is identified in the Stage Plan.

2. Confirm with the Chairman that the product is ready for review. This should occur several days prior to the planned review date to allow for preparation time.

3. Confirm the attendees with the Chairman and the Project Assurance Team.

4. Agree with the Chairman and Reviewers the length of preparation time needed and review location.

5. Assess the Question Lists from the Reviewers, identifying any errors in the product which can be agreed without further discussion.

6. Agree the agenda with the Chairman in the light of the Question Lists.

Review

1. Answer any questions about the product.

2. Offer an opinion to the Chairman on whether a question has highlighted an error in the product.

3. If the review is judged to be complete, collect from the Chairman the Follow-Up Action List and any annotated copies of the product from the Reviewers.

Follow-Up

1. Resolve all allocated action items.

2. Obtain sign-off for each action item from the nominated Reviewers.

3. If an action item cannot be resolved within the time allowed, the Chairman and Producer may decide to transfer it to a Project Issue.

4. Inform the Chairman if the resolution of the action items cannot be completed within the time allowed and agree new target dates.

5. Pass the Follow-Up Action List to the Chairman on resolution of all the action items.

REVIEWER RESPONSIBILITIES

Preparation

1. Consult the Product Description and any pertinent checklists and standards against which the product should be judged.

2. Allow sufficient time to prepare for the review.

3. Consult any necessary source documents from which the product is derived.

4. Annotate any spelling or typographical mistakes on the product copy, but do not add these to the Question List.

5. Check the product for completeness, defects, ambiguities, inconsistencies, lack of clarity or deviations from standards. Note any such items on the Question List.

6. Forward the Question List to the Producer in advance of the review. If possible, this should be done early enough to give the Producer time to digest the points and prepare an agenda with the Chairman.

7. Forward a Question List and the annotated product copy to the Chairman if unable to attend the review.

Review

1. Ensure that the points noted on the Question List are raised at the review.

2. Restrict comments to faults in the product under review.

3. Avoid attempting to redesign the product.

4. Avoid 'improvement' comments if the product meets requirements and standards.

5. Verify and approve the Follow-Up Action List as complete and correct when read back by the Chairman.

6. Agree to assist in the resolution of any action items if requested by the Chairman.

7. Request to check and sign off any action items either raised personally or which impact the Reviewer's area of expertise or interest.

Follow-Up

1.   Work with the Producer to resolve any allocated action item.

2.   Check and sign off those action items where allocated as Reviewer.

Formal and Informal Reviews

Quality Reviews can be either formal (i.e. a scheduled meeting conducted as described above) or informal (i.e. a 'get-together' between two people to informally walk through a product). Informal Quality Reviews will follow a similar format to the Formal Quality Review – the paperwork emerging from both meetings is similar. The main difference will be the informality of the proceedings during the three phases and the overall time required.

For informal Quality Reviews two people can be given the task of checking each other's work on an on-going basis. Alternatively an experienced person can be asked to regularly hold reviews of an inexperienced person's work as it develops.

Factors in deciding whether a formal or informal review is needed are:

- The importance of the product

- Is it a final deliverable?

- Is it the source for a number of other products?

- The author's experience

- Who is the product's consumer?

- Is it a review of a partial document?

Summary

The PRINCE Quality Review technique is a structured way of running a meeting to ensure that all aspects are properly covered. It needs to be used with common sense to avoid the dangers of an over-bureaucratic approach but with an intent to follow the procedures laid down (to ensure nothing is missed).

11 | Configuration Management

What is Configuration Management?

The objective of configuration management is to achieve a controlled and traceable product evolution through properly authorised specifications, design, software, hardware and reports.

This objective is met by defining and ensuring:

- The issue and control of properly authorised design documents

- The issue and control of properly authorised changes to the design documents

- The control of the baselines of a product and their relationship with the actual as-built state.

Configuration management is also the process of managing change to the elements which comprise a product. It implies that any version of the product and any revision of the modules which make up the product can be retrieved at any time, and that the resulting product will always be built in an identical manner. Product enhancements and special variants create the need to control multiple versions and releases of the product. All these have to be handled by configuration management.

Put in PRINCE terms, configuration management is a discipline which:

- Records what sub-products are required in order to build a product

- Provides identifiers and version numbers to all products

- Controls access and change to components of a product once they have been declared complete by the developer

- Provides information on the impact of possible changes

- Keeps information on the links between the various parts of a product, i.e. what components comprise a sub-product, where is module x used, of what does the 'full product' consist

- Provides information on the status of products (Configuration Items) being developed, including who is responsible

- Is the sensible storage place for Product Descriptions

- Gives project management the assurance that products are being developed in the correct sequence.

Why do it?

'If the product you develop has more than one version, more than a few components or more than one person working on it, you are doing configuration management. The only question is how well you are doing it.'

Configuration management holds a central position in PRINCE. The identified Configuration Items and their life cycles provide the information for the Product Breakdown Structures. The links allow the construction of the Product Flow Diagrams. They offer input and verification of the products required for a plan. You cannot adequately do change control without configuration management. It provides product copies and Product Descriptions for quality checks and keeps track of the status of the product. It provides the information to construct a release package, either a complete one or a partial one, and then records the issue of a release.

Configuration Items are valuable assets in themselves. Configuration management helps management know what its assets are supposed to be, who is reponsible for their safekeeping and whether the actual inventory matches the official one.

Configuration management gives control over the versions of products in use, identifies products affected by any problems, and makes it easier to assess the impact of changes.

Configuration management supports the production of information on problem trends, such as which products are being changed regularly, thereby assisting in the proactive prevention of problems.

Where the end-product is to be used in more than one place, configuration management helps organisations to control the distribution of changes to these operational sites. Where there is any volume of changes, there will be the need to decide between putting together a 'release package' of several changes or issuing a complete new product. The latter may be a more controlled and cost-effective means of updating an operational product than sending out one changed product at a time. The decision and control mechanisms for this are part of configuration management.

Configuration management supports the maintenance of information on proven, reliable releases to which products can revert in case of problems.

Because all products are under the control of configuration management once they have been developed, it makes it more difficult for them to be changed maliciously, thus improving security.

The data held in the Configuration Library helps to recreate a release after any disaster by identifying the products required and their storage place.

Coverage

Configuration management covers all the technical products of a project. It can also be used to record and store management and quality products, such as plans, quality check details and approvals to proceed. Whether management products are included or not depends on such factors as:

- Effort involved
- Resource availability
- Capability of any other current method for handling management and quality products
- Project manager's preference
- Availability of CM software.

Costs

There are the expected costs of staffing and training Configuration Librarians. If a central office (say part of a Project Support Office) has been set up to provide configuration management functions to a number of projects, there may be a need for a Configuration Manager.

If software is to be used to record and track the data, there will be the cost of its purchase or rental, any hardware bought to run it, plus the staff training. Having said that, it is very difficult to keep the comprehensive records required to do a complete job without a computer database and software. The costs here are far outweighed by the increase in speed, capacity and detail of information. The increase in speed of reaction by the Configuration Librarian probably reduces the number of librarians needed to cover all the site's products.

The need to go through the configuration management tasks may slow down slightly the hand-over of a finished item or the implementation of a change. But this penalty is very small when weighed against the risk and impact of using operationally a product or sub-product which is from an incorrect release, or has not been checked out. Without it there is also the risk of more than one person changing a product simultaneously, resulting in all but the final change being lost.

Possible Problems

If products are defined at too low a level, the Configuration Librarian may be overwhelmed by the amount of data to be fed into the library. This is particularly a problem where no configuration management software is being used.

If products are defined at too high a level, the information for impact analysis may be too vague and result in a larger than necessary product change being indicated, e.g. altering a whole set of products when only one sub-product is affected.

Procedures must cater for emergency changes, where an emergency change is required in order to let the operational product continue.

Where configuration management is new, development staff may be tempted to view its controls as bottlenecks and bureaucracy. But it has been used in engineering for many years and is regarded in those circles as essential. It is also regarded as an essential part of any quality product, should you be looking for accreditation under such standards as ISO 9001. It is regarded as essential because of the control it gives and the experience over many years which has shown its value and the cost of problems arising when it is not used.

When is it done?

A configuration management plan is required as part of the Project Initiation Document. This should state:

- What method is to be used

- Who has the responsibility for configuration management

- What naming convention will be used to identify products of this project

- What types of product are to be covered

- What types of status are to be used (e.g. 'allocated', 'draft available', 'quality checked')

- What method of change control will be used.

Once a product has been identified as required, it should receive an identifier from the configuration management method. This often coincides with the creation of a draft Product Description.

Among the configuration management planning activities required are those to identify what baselines will be required and for what purpose, which can exist concurrently and which cannot, and when baselines will be taken.

The status of a product should be tracked from the moment the Product Description is created.

Configuration Item Attributes

The detail to be kept about the products will depend to some extent on the complexity of the end-product, the number of products, the resource available to keep the records and the information demanded by the maintenance and support groups.

Below is a list of potential information about a product which should be considered against the needs of the project.

Part number
> A unique configuration identifier allocated by either the configuration management software or the librarian.

Title
> The name of the product.

Purpose; Composition; Format; Quality criteria; Quality check method
> These five fields are those from a Product Description and contain exactly the same information.

Checklist identity
> Reference to a checklist which would help check the quality of the product.

Provided by
> If from an external source.

Current version
> Number of this particular version of the product. This is usually linked to a baseline. You may wish to divide this into version and sub-version number, if you want to use, for example, '3.1'.

Category
> This can identify the category of product, such as hardware, software, electrical, packing, documentation, etc.

Type
> This usually amplifies 'category'. It might define the model, type of hardware, operating product, manual, education material and so on. It might also be used to identify documents as design, source code.

Variant
> A product which has the same basic functionality as another product, but is different in some small way. An example would be another country's currency symbol.

Serial number or software reference
> The serial number of a device or bought-in package.

Location
> Where the product is physically kept.

Status

Current status of the configuration item. You might have your own ideas on the possible entries for this, but the following list may give you some extra ideas:

Product not defined

Product description in progress

Product description written

Product description approved

Product ordered

Product in progress

Draft version available

Product in test

Product under review

Product approved

Product accepted

Product delivered

Product installed

Product under change.

Not all of these need be used, just those which fit your status needs.

Start date of the current status

Forecast or actual date of the next status change

Project stage in which it will be developed

Responsible officer

Who is responsible for production of the product.

Start date of this responsibility

End date of the responsibility

Parent

The accepted meaning is that if a product has several parts, the product is the *parent* and the parts *children*. Another general rule is that a *child* can have only one *parent*, even if it is used elsewhere.

Child

> The reverse of the above, showing links to whatever its *child* component items are.

Used in

> Apart from the one *parent*, this identifies any other item of which it forms a part.

Uses

> Links to other items which form part of it, but of which it is not the *parent*.

Change

> Cross-references to the Issue Log entry or entries which affect it.

Quality Log

> Cross-reference to the Quality Log where information about the quality check of the product is held.

The Product Description should be filed in the Quality Log. If you do this, the Product Description entries described above may not be needed. But an alternative is to use software to keep it as part of the CM database.

Baselines

Baselines are moments in a product's evolution when it and all its components have reached an acceptable state, such that they can be 'frozen' and used as a base for the next step. The next step may be to release the product to the user, or it may be that you have 'frozen' a design and will now construct the sub-products.

Products constantly evolve and are subject to change as a project moves through its life cycle and, later on, in the operational life of the product. A Project Manager will need to know the answer to many questions, such as:

- What is the latest agreed level of specification to which we are working?

- What exact design are we implementing?

- What did we release to site x last January?

In other words, a frozen picture of what products and what versions of them constituted a certain situation. These frozen pictures are known as **baselines**.

A baseline may be defined as a set of known and agreed configuration items under change control from which further progress can be charted. This description indicates that you will baseline only products which represent either the entire product or at least a significant sub-product.

A baseline is created for one of a number of reasons:

- A sound base for future work

- As a point to which you can retreat if development goes wrong

- An indication of the component and version numbers of a release

- A bill of material showing the variants released to a specific site

- To copy the products and documentation at the current baseline to all remote sites

- A standard configuration (e.g. product description) against which supplies can be obtained (e.g. purchase of personal computers for a group)

- The state the product must reach before it can be released or upgraded

- Comparison of one baseline against another in terms of the products contained and their versions

- Transfer to another library

- The obtaining of a report on what products of the baseline are not of status 'x'.

The baseline record itself should be a product, so that it can be controlled in the same way as other products. It is a baseline identifier, date, reason and list of all the products and their version numbers which comprise that baseline. Because of its different format it is often held in a separate file.

Status Accounting and Auditing

Configuration status accounting provides a complete statement of the current status and history of the products generated within the project. Configuration auditing checks whether the recorded description of products matches their physical representation and whether items have been built to their specification.

CONFIGURATION STATUS ACCOUNTING

The purpose of this is to provide a report on:

- The status of one or all Configuration Items

- All the events which have impacted those products.

This allows comparison with the plans and provides tracking of changes to products.

In order to provide this information it is necessary for the configuration management method to record all the transactions affecting each Configuration Item. At the simplest level this means that we can tell the status of each item and version. If we can afford to keep complete records, our library will have broken the specification down into parts, which are linked to design items, which in turn link to constructed modules. All approved changes to any one of these will show the linkages and dates of any amendment, plus the baselines incorporating the changes. Our records will show who was responsible and possibly the costs.

For the purpose of status accounting the configuration management method should be able to produce reports on such things as:

- What is the history of development of a particular item

- How many Requests For Change were approved last month

- Who is responsible for this item

- What items in the design baseline have been changed since it was approved

- On what items have changes been approved but not yet implemented.

CONFIGURATION AUDITING

The purpose of configuration auditing is to account for the differences between a delivered product and its original agreed specification. In other words, can the records trace a path from the original specification through any approved changes to what a product looks like now. These audits should verify that:

- All authorised versions of configuration items exist

- Only authorised configuration items exist

- All change records, release records have been properly authorised by project management

- Implemented changes are as authorised.

In PRINCE terms, this is defined as an inspection of the recorded Configuration Item Description and the current representation of that item to ensure that the latter matches its current specification, and that the specification of each item is consistent with that of its parent in the structure. In a sense, it can be regarded as similar to stock control. Does the book description match with what we have on the shelf? In addition the audit should ensure that documentation is complete and that project standards have been met.

In engineering establishments, the aim of configuration auditing is to check that, in spite of changes which may have taken place in requirements and design, the items produced conform to the latest agreed specification and that quality review procedures have been performed satisfactorily. This is done by verifying at successive baselines that the item produced at each baseline conforms to the specification produced for it in the previous baseline plus any approved changes.

Configuration audits should be done:

- Shortly after implementation of a new configuration management product

- Before and after major changes to the structure of the project's end product

- After disasters such as the loss of records

- On detection of any 'rash' of unauthorised configuration items

- Randomly.

CONFIGURATION AUDIT CHECKLIST

Here is an example checklist for an audit. The following items should be examined:

- Do the configuration records match the physical items?

- Random approved changes – are they recorded in the Issue Log? Are they linked to the appropriate products? Is their implementation controlled by the configuration management method?

- Random products – is the library up-to-date and accurate? Are there links to relevant Project Issues?

- Are regular configuration audits carried out? Are the results recorded? Have follow actions been performed?

- Random products – are archived and back-up versions of products retained and recorded in the correct manner?

- Are the recorded versions of products used in multiple locations correct?

- Do product names and version numbers meet naming conventions?

- Is library housekeeping carried out in accordance with defined procedures?

- Are staff adequately trained?

- Can baselines be easily and accurately created, recreated and used?

Building a Release Package

At the end of a project the product which has been developed is released into production. For many installations this may be a simple matter. The product will run operationally on the same hardware used for its development, and 'release' is nothing more than moving the object code and any control language procedures to new libraries (and sometimes not even that!).

But there are many problems concerned with the move of development work over to live operation:

- How do we release details of how to build the product to a sister company on another site?

- How do we ensure that we only release products which have been thoroughly tested as part of the whole product?

- How do we create innumerable copies of the product (like a software house) and guarantee that they will be identical?

- How can we change an operational product without the risk of it malfunctioning after the change?

- How can we keep a check on which of our customers or sites has what version of the product?

- How do we install a major enhancement of a product?

- If the people who developed the product are not to be the people who install the product, how do they know how to do it?

- Do we issue the complete product for every update or just the changes?

- Do we issue a complete new user/operations manual or only the changed pages?

The answer is in release control, another important job for the Configuration Librarian. The tasks for the librarian are:

- Identify the products to be included in the release

- Ensure that all the required products have reached a status which allows them to be released into live operation

- Report on any required products which do not have a current approved status

- Build a release package

- List the changes since the previous release

- Distribute the release

- Be able to recreate any baseline (i.e. past release) if a site reports problems on an earlier release

- Know which site has what version and variant of the product.

CONTROL OF RELEASES

Each product release should have a release identifier of the same form as the version number described for a product, i.e. *baseline number.issue number*, which identifies:

- The level of functionality provide by the release – defined by the baseline number

- The modification status of the release – defined by the issue number

- The release configuration – by reference to the relevant baseline summary.

Revision of release and issue number

The release identifier should be revised:

- When the new release of the product provides changed functionality – the baseline number is incremented up to the next whole number (e.g. 2.1 becomes 3.0)

- When the new release of the product provides fault fixes only – the issue number is incremented by one (e.g. 1.4 becomes 1.5)

- *Optionally* when the new release of the product consolidates many (e.g. 20) minor changes – the baseline number is incremented up to the next whole number.

Release package contents

A release should be accompanied by a release build summary. It should contain:

- The release name and identifier

- The release date

- The person/section/group with responsibility for the release. This will normally also be the contact for any installation problems. If not then this information should be added

- A brief description of the release, whether it is a complete or partial release, what has caused the release, what is its purpose, the major benefits over previous releases

- A list of prerequisites for the installation of the release

- A list of all the Project Issues answered by this release

- A bill of material, listing what is contained in the release. This should cover documentation and any procedures

- Assembly steps

- Assembly test steps

- Any customisation steps. If the release can be tailored in any way, this describes the possibilities and lists the steps to be carried out

- Notification of any dates when support for previous releases will cease

- An acknowledgement to be completed and returned by the assembler on successful completion of the assembly.

While current, a baseline cannot be changed. It remains active until it is superseded by the next baseline.

12 | Change Control

The Need for Control

No matter how well planned a project has been, if there is no control over changes, this will destroy any chance of bringing the project in on schedule and to budget. In any project there will be changes for many reasons:

- Government legislation has changed and this must be reflected in the system specification

- The users change their mind on what is wanted

- Because the development cycle is making the user think more and more about the product, extra features suggest themselves for inclusion

- There is a merge of departments, change of responsibilities, company merger or take-over which radically alters the Project Definition

- The supplier finds that it will be impossible to deliver everything within the agreed schedule or cost

- The supplier cannot meet an acceptance criterion, such as performance

- A product delivered by an outside contractor or another system fails to meet its specification.

All of these need a technique to control them and their effect on the project. This technique must make sure they are not ignored, but that nothing is implemented of which the appropriate level of management is unaware. This includes the Project Board. In PRINCE 2 all possible changes are handled by the Change Control technique. Apart from controlling possible changes, it provides a formal entry point through which all points can be raised. It is a connecting link between Quality Reviews and the rest of the project:

- Where an error is found during Quality Review which belongs to a different product than the one under review

- Where work to correct an error found during Quality Review cannot be done during the agreed Follow-Up period.

Project Issues

There are three types of Project Issue in PRINCE 2:

- Project Issues

- Requests For Change

- Off-Specifications.

They are used to record desired change to, or some failure in, the project's products. If the role is used, it is sensible to make part of the Configuration Librarian's role the control of Project Issues. This is assumed throughout the rest of this chapter. If there is no Configuration Librarian, the responsibility rests with the Project Manager.

PROJECT ISSUE

A Project Issue is the formal way into a project of any enquiry, complaint or request outside the scope of a Quality Review Question List. It can be raised by anyone associated with the project about anything, for example:

- A desired new or changed function

- A failure of a product in meeting some aspect of the user requirements. In such cases the report should be accompanied by evidence of the failure and, where appropriate, sufficient material to allow someone to recreate the failure

- A question about a possible misunderstanding

- A problem with a plan

- A failure of communication.

In other words, there is no limit to the content of a Project Issue beyond the fact that it should be about the project. Any error found during a Quality

Review normally goes on an Action List. The exception is if an error is detected in a product which is not the one being reviewed. Such errors are put onto a Project Issue as the way of getting them into the change control system.

When considering the procedures for handling Project Issues, there is the possibility that the subject will be outside the scope of the project. An example might be a fault in a component which is used in many products across the department. Although it is being used in the project it clearly has a wider implication. There should be a procedure to close the issue off as far as the project is concerned and transfer it to a departmental level. The same approach applies if the project is part of a programme and an error is found in a Quality Review which affects other projects in the programme.

The Configuration Librarian will log receipt of the Project Issue, allocate the unique identifier, and pass a copy back to the originator and to each member of the Project Assurance Team. The Project Issue is now classed as 'Open'.

All unresolved Project Issues are reviewed at regular meetings, called and chaired by the Project Manager and attended by the Project Assurance Team. The issues are evaluated with the aim of making recommendations to the Project Manager on their resolution. The outcome is normally one of the following:

- The issue has been raised due to a misunderstanding by the originator. The misunderstanding should be explained to the originator and the issue closed

- The issue is proposing a change to a baselined Configuration Item. The Project Issue is a Request For Change

- The issue requests a change to the agreed user specification, acceptance criteria or a Product Description. The Project Issue is a Request For Change

- A product does not meet its specification. The Project Issue is an Off-Specification

- More evaluation is required

- The issue was received too recently for any evaluation.

The frequency of such meetings will depend on the volume of issues being received, but it should be held regularly and with sufficient frequency to ensure that no inordinate delay occurs in taking action. The Project Manager decides on the action to take on Project Issues based on the recommendations of the Project Assurance Team.

All Project Issue have to be closed by the end of the project. It can only be closed in the ways mentioned in the recommendations above.

REQUEST FOR CHANGE

A Request For Change records a proposed modification to the user requirements.

The Request For Change requires analysis to see how much work is involved. This is normally done by senior team members with the appropriate skills and experience. Part of this work is called impact analysis, where the Configuration Librarian helps to identify what other products or Configuration Items will be affected. It is particularly important that the librarian identifies any baselined Configuration Items which will need to change. This is because the Project Board have already been told of the completion of those items. Any change to such items must be approved by the Project Board.

The identified work is costed and the impact on the stage plan's budget and schedule assessed. For the next decision the Project Manager will want to know if any of the work could be done within the tolerance levels of the current plan. For this reason it is best that a batch of requests are studied, to give a wider view of the effect on the plans.

In preparation for the next decision, the Requests For Change have to be awarded a priority rating. This can be one of four:

- High
- Medium
- Low
- Cosmetic.

It should be the job of the Senior User to provide the priority rating and canvass the users.

In order for the Request For Change to be implemented, it must be approved by either the Project Manager or the Project Board whose decision it is depends on the following:

- If it is not a change to a Configuration Item which has already been baselined and the work can be done within the current plan's tolerances, the Project Manager can make the decision to implement it. Alternatively it can be passed to the Project Board for its decision. Since experience shows that there will be a lot of changes during the project, it is a good idea to make the Project Board decide on any changes other than trivialities. This keeps the board aware of how many changes are being requested and their cumulative impact on the schedule and cost. If the stage plan runs into trouble later, it is usually too late for the Project Manager to get any sympathy about a claim that lots of requests have been actioned without asking for more time or money. The answer will usually be 'Why didn't you ask us? We could have cancelled or delayed some of them.'

- If the change is to one or more Configuration Items which the Project Board have already been told are complete (to any baseline, not necessarily the final one), the decision must be made by the Project Board. More than anything, this is to retain the confidence level of the board. If it has been told that something is finished and later find out that it has been changed without consultation, its sense of being in control evaporates.

- If the work to do the Request For Change cannot be done within the tolerance levels of the current Stage Plan, the decision on action must come from the Project Board. The Project Manager must submit an Exception Plan with the Request For Change, showing the new schedule and cost for the rest of the stage.

- The Senior User on the Project Board is the key role in its decisions on whether to implement the changes. The Configuration Librarian therefore passes to the Senior User all those Requests For Change which have not been decided by the Project Manager. It is the Senior User's job to put them in order of priority for consideration by the board.

The Project Board's decision may be to:

- Implement the change. If the change required an Exception Plan, then this means approving the Exception Plan

- Delay the change to an enhancement project after the current one is finished

- Defer a decision until a later meeting

- Ask for more information

- Cancel the request.

The decision should be documented on the request and the Issue Log.

Whenever its status changes, a copy should be sent to the originator.

The Project Manager is responsible for scheduling any approved changes. This work will possibly involve the issue of a copy of one or more products by the Configuration Librarian.

On receipt of a completed Request For Change the Configuration Librarian should ensure that any amended products have been re-submitted to the configuration library. The Quality File should be updated with the finalised request, the log annotated and the originator advised.

OFF-SPECIFICATION

An Off-Specification is used to document any situation where the system fails to meet its specification in some respect.

The Configuration Librarian allocates the next unique Project Issue identifier from the log, sends a copy of the issue to its author. Senior team members with the help of the Configuration Librarian carry out an impact analysis to discover which products are affected by the Off-Specification, and then assesses the effort needed. If it is discovered that the Off-Specification has been raised in error, and should have been a Request For Change, the Project Issue is suitably commented. The Issue Log is updated and the originator informed.

As with Requests For Change, the decision on action is taken by either the Project Manager or Project Board:

- If the Off-Specification does not involve a change to a Configuration Item which has already been baselined and the work can be done within the current plan's tolerances, the Project Manager can make the decision to implement it

- If the Off-Specification requires changes to one or more Configuration Items which the Project Board have already been told are complete (to any baseline, not necessarily the final one), the decision must be made by the Project Board

- If the work to do the Off-Specification cannot be done within the tolerance levels of the current Stage Plan, the decision on action must come from the Project Board. The Project Manager must submit an Exception Plan with the Off-Specification Report, showing the new schedule and cost for the rest of the stage.

The Project Board's decision may be to:

- Correct the fault. If the work required an Exception Plan, then this means approving the Exception Plan.

- Delay correction of the fault to an enhancement project after the current one is finished

- Defer a decision until a later meeting

- Ask for more information.

The decision should be documented on the Off-Specification and the Issue Log, and an updated copy filed. Whenever its status changes, a copy should be sent to the originator.

The Project Manager is responsible for scheduling any approved work to correct Off-Specifications. This work will possibly involve the issue of a copy of one or more products by the Configuration Librarian.

On receipt of a corrected Off-Specification the Configuration Librarian should ensure that any amended products have been re-submitted to the configuration library. The Issue Log should be updated with the final details and the originator advised.

The Quality File

There is one Quality File for each PRINCE project. It is the responsibility of the Project Manager. If a Configuration Librarian has been appointed to the project it is important that the duties with regard to the Quality File are clearly defined between this role and the Project Manager. Normally the Configuration Librarian will be allocated the duties of logging and filing all the documents.

The Quality File contains the Quality Log and the forms which are produced as part of the quality controls applied during the life of the project. It is an important part of the audit trail which can be followed by the user or an independent Quality Assurance body to assess what quality checking has been carried out and how effective it has been. As such, it is a deliverable product.

Wherever possible, the originals of documents should be filed in the Quality File. A copy can be filed if the original has to be circulated for signature or comments, but on its return the original should be replaced in the Quality File.

The Quality File should have sections for:

Quality Log

Each quality check should have a uniques number to provide the basis for statistics on how many quality checks have been carried out.

Quality Review Invitations

On filing this document there should be a check that there is no unreported date slippage compared to the planned review date. If there is, the Project Manager should be notified.

Quality Review Results

When all corrective actions on the Action List have been taken and the list signed off by the Chairman of the review, it is filed in the Quality File. If the review was terminated prematurely, the review documents such as Follow-Up Action List, annotated product copies, Question Lists should all be filed here in the Quality File.

Issue Log

Appendix: Product Descriptions

The following Appendix contains suggested Product Descriptions for the PRINCE 2 management and quality products. Care should be taken to scrutinise them and tune them to any site or project's specific needs.

One non-standard entry has been added to the Product Descriptions. 'Processes Involved' will to help link the product to the process(es) where it would be developed. This information is for the benefit of the reader of this book, and should be removed before using the Product Description in a project.

Title: Acceptance Criteria

PURPOSE

A definition in measurable terms of those aspects of the final product which it must demonstrate for the product to be acceptable to the customer and staff who will be affected by the product.

COMPOSITION

Criteria suitable for the product, such as:

- Target dates
- Major functions
- Performance levels
- Capacity
- Accuracy
- Appearance
- Availability
- Reliability
- Development cost
- Running costs
- Maintenance
- Security
- Ease of use
- Timings
- Personnel level required to use/operate the product.

FORM(AT)

List of acceptance criteria, measurements, dates by when each criterion should be met, including any interim measurements and dates.

DERIVATION

- Background information
- Project Mandate
- Project Brief
- Senior User.

Processes Involved

Acceptance Criteria may be in the original Project Mandate or should be developed as part of the Project Brief in the process 'Start Up the Project' (SU).

Quality Criteria

- All criteria are measurable
- Each criterion is individually realistic
- The criteria as a group are realistic, e.g. high quality, early delivery and low cost may not go together.

Quality Method

Formal Quality Review between Project Manager and those with assurance responsibilities.

Title: Business Case

Purpose

To document the reasons and justification for undertaking a project, based on the estimated cost of development and the anticipated business benefits to be gained. The on-going viability of the project will be monitored by the Project Board against the Business Case.

The Business Case may include legal or legislative reasons why the project is needed.

Composition

- Business reasons for undertaking the project
- Business benefits to be gained from development of the product
- Development cost and time scale
- Investment Appraisal.

(These may refer to the overall Business Case if it is part of a programme.)

Form(at)

Document to standard site practice with the composition shown above.

DERIVATION

Information for the Business Case is derived from:

- Project Mandate/Project Brief (reasons)
- Project Plan (costs)
- The customer.

PROCESSES INVOLVED

The existence of a provisional Business Case is checked during the process 'Start Up the Project' (SU). If the Project Mandate does not contain a Business Case, an outline of this would be created during 'Start Up the Project' as part of the Project Brief. The Business Case is finalised during the process 'Initiate the Project' (IP).

QUALITY CRITERIA

- Can the benefits be justified?
- Do the cost and time scale match those in the Project Plan?
- Are the reasons for the project consistent with corporate or programme strategy?

QUALITY METHOD

Quality Review with the Executive and anyone appointed to business assurance.

Title: Checkpoint Report

PURPOSE

To report at a frequency defined in the Project Initiation Document the progress and status of work for a team.

COMPOSITION

- Date of the checkpoint
- Period covered by the report
- Report on any follow-up action from previous reports
- Products completed during the period
- Quality work carried out during the period

- Products to be completed during the next period
- Risk assessment
- Business Case review
- Other actual or potential problems or deviations from plan

FORM(AT)

According to the agreement between the Project Manager and the Project Board, the report may be verbal or written. It should contain the information given above, plus any extra data requested by the Project Board.

DERIVATION

- Stage Plan actuals and forecasts
- Risk Log
- Business Case
- Team member reports.

PROCESSES INVOLVED

Checkpoint Reports will be generated as part of the process 'Execute Work Package' (MP2) and/or 'Control the Stage' (CS) at a frequency defined during Project Initiation (PI).

QUALITY CRITERIA

- Every team member's work covered.
- Includes an update on any unresolved problems from the previous report.
- Does it reflect the Stage or Team Plan situation?
- Does it reflect any significant change to the Risk Log?
- Does it reflect any significant change to the Business Case?
- Does it reflect any change in a team member's package delivery which has an impact on others?

QUALITY METHOD

Informal check by the Team Manager and those with assurance responsibilities.

Title: End Project Report

PURPOSE

The report is the Project Manager's report to the Project Board (which may pass it on to corporate or programme management) on how the project has performed against the intentions stated in its Project Initiation Document and revised during the project life cycle. It should cover comparisons with the original targets, planned cost, schedule and tolerances, the revised Business Case and final version of the Project Plan.

COMPOSITION

- Assessment of the achievement of the project's objectives
- Performance against the planned (and revised) target times and costs
- The effect on the original Project Plan and Business Case of any changes which were approved
- Final statistics on change issues received during the project and the total impact (time, money, benefits, for example) of any approved changes
- Statistics for all quality work carried out
- Post Implementation Review date and plan.

FORM(AT)

To the defined site standard for reports with the above content plus any extra information requested by the Project Board.

DERIVATION

- The final Project Plan with actuals
- The Project Initiation Document
- Issue Log.

PROCESSES INVOLVED

The End Project Report is produced during the process 'Close the Project' (CP).

QUALITY CRITERIA

- Does the report describe the impact of any approved changes on the original intentions stated in the Project Initiation Document?
- Does the report cover all the benefits which can be assessed at this time?
- Does the quality work done during the project meet the quality expectations of the Customer?

QUALITY METHOD

Formal quality review between Project Manager and those with assurance responsibilities.

Title: End Stage Report

PURPOSE

The purpose of the End Stage Report is to report on a stage which has just completed, the overall project situation and sufficient information to ask for a Project Board decision on the next step to take with the project.

The Project Board use the information in the End Stage Report to approve the next stage plan, amend the project scope and ask for a revised next stage plan, or stop the project.

Normally the End Stage Report for the last stage of a project is combined with the End Project Report.

COMPOSITION

- Current Stage Plan with all the actuals
- Project Plan outlook
- Business Case review
- Risk review
- Project Issue situation
- Quality checking statistics
- Report on any internal or external events which have affected stage performance.

FORM(AT)

Site report standards covering the information described above plus any extra requested by the Project Board.

DERIVATION

Information for the report is obtained from:

- The Stage Plan and actuals
- The next Stage Plan (if appropriate)
- The updated Project Plan
- The embryo Lessons Learned Report
- Data from the Quality Log
- Completed Work Package data.

PROCESSES INVOLVED

The End Stage Report is an output from the process 'Manage Stage Boundaries' (SB).

QUALITY CRITERIA

- Does it clearly describe stage performance against the plan?
- Were any approved modifications described, together with their impact?
- Does it give an accurate picture of the quality testing work done in the stage?
- Does it give an accurate review of the revised risk situation?
- Does it give an accurate assessment of the ability of the project to meet its Business Case?

QUALITY METHOD

Informal Quality Review between the Project Manager and those with assurance responsibilities.

Title: Exception Report

PURPOSE

An Exception Report is produced when costs and/or time scales for an approved Stage Plan are forecast to exceed the tolerance levels set. It is sent by the Project Manager in order to appraise the Project Board of the adverse situation.

An Exception Report will normally result in the Project Board asking the Project Manager to produce an Exception Plan.

COMPOSITION

- A description of the cause of the deviation from the Stage Plan
- The consequences of the deviation
- The available options
- The effect of each option on the Business Case, risks, project and stage tolerances
- The Project Manager's recommendations.

FORM(AT)

Site report standard containing the information shown above.

DERIVATION

The information for an Exception Report is drawn from:

- Current stage plan and actuals
- Project plan and actuals
- Deviation forecast
- Issue Log
- Risk Log
- Quality Log
- Checkpoint Reports
- Project Board advice of an external event which affects the project.

PROCESSES INVOLVED

An Exception Report is output from the process 'Escalate Project Issues' (CS8).

QUALITY CRITERIA

- The Exception Report must accurately show the current status of stage and project budget and schedule, plus the forecast impact on both of the deviation
- The reason(s) for the deviation must be stated
- Options, including 'do nothing' must be put forward, together with their impact on objectives, plans, Business Case and risks
- A recommendation must be made.

QUALITY METHOD

Informal review between the Project Manager, any Team Managers and those with assurance responsibilities.

Title: Highlight Report

PURPOSE

For the Project Manager to provide the Project Board with a summary of the stage status at intervals defined by them.

A Highlight Report normally covers a series of Checkpoint Reports. The Project Board uses the report to monitor stage and project progress. The Project Manager also uses it to advise the Project Board of any potential problems or areas where the Project Board could help.

COMPOSITION

- Date
- Project
- Stage
- Period covered
- Budget status
- Schedule status
- Products completed during the period

- Actual or potential problems
- Products to be completed during the next period
- Project Issue status
- Budget and schedule impact of any changes approved so far in the stage.

FORM(AT)

Site reporting standards containing the above information plus any extra data requested by the Project Board.

DERIVATION

Information for the Highlight Reports is derived from:

- Checkpoint Reports
- Stage Plan
- Issue Log
- Risk Log.

PROCESSES INVOLVED

Highlight Reports are output from the process 'Report Highlights' (CS6).

QUALITY CRITERIA

- Accurate reflection of Checkpoint Reports
- Accurate summary of the Issue Log status
- Accurate summary of the Stage Plan status
- Highlights any potential problem areas.

QUALITY METHOD

Informal review between the Project Manager and those with assurance responsibilities.

Title: Project Issue

PURPOSE

To record any matter which has to be brought to the attention of the project, and requires an answer. A Project Issue may be a:

- Request For Change
- Off-Specification
- Question
- Statement of concern.

COMPOSITION

- Author
- Date
- Issue number
- Description of the issue
- Priority
- Impact analysis
- Decision
- Signature of decision maker(s)
- Date of decision.

FORM(AT)

Department style of form with the headings shown under 'Composition'.

DERIVATION

Anyone may submit a Project Issue. Typical sources are users and specialists working on the project, the Project Manager and those with assurance responsibilities.

PROCESSES INVOLVED

The process 'Capture Project Issues' (CS3) deals with collating Project Issues. They are then examined during the process 'Examine Project Issues' (CS4).

QUALITY CRITERIA

- Is the statement of the problem/requirement clear?
- Has all necessary information been made available?
- Have all the implications been considered?
- Has the Project Issue been correctly logged?

QUALITY METHOD

Check by the person responsible for the Issue Log.

Title: Issue Log

PURPOSE

The purpose of the Issue Log is to:

- Allocate a unique number to each Project Issue
- Record the type of Project Issue
- Be a summary of the Project Issues, their analysis and status.

COMPOSITION

- Project Issue number
- Project Issue type (Issue, Request For Change, Off-Specification)
- Author
- Date created
- Date of last update
- Status.

FORM(AT)

Standard department form with the headings shown under 'Composition'.

DERIVATION

Project Issues may be raised by anyone associated with the project at any time.

PROCESSES INVOLVED

The entry of an issue on the Issue Log occurs in process 'Capture Project Issues' (CS3). Issue status may be updated in process 'Examine Project Issues' (CS4).

QUALITY CRITERIA

- Does the status indicate whether action has been taken?
- Are the Project Issues uniquely identified, including to which product they refer?
- Is access to the Issue Log controlled?
- Is the Issue Log kept in a safe place?

QUALITY METHOD

Regular inspection.

Title: Lessons Learned Report

PURPOSE

The purpose of the Lessons Learned Report is to pass on to other projects any useful lessons which can be learned from this project.

The data in the report should be used by an independent group, such as quality assurance, who are responsible for the site Quality Management System, to refine, change and improve project management and technical standards. Statistics on how much effort was needed for products can help improve future estimating.

COMPOSITION

- What management and quality processes:
  - went well
  - went badly
  - were lacking
- An assessment of the efficacy of technical methods and tools used
- Recommendations for future enhancement or modification of the project management method, including the reasons
- Measurements on how much effort was required to create the various products

- A description of any abnormal events causing deviations to targets or plans
- An analysis of Project Issues raised, their causes and results
- Statistics on how effective Quality Reviews and other tests were in error trapping (e.g. how many errors were found after products had passed a Quality Review or test).

FORM(AT)

Site reporting standards containing at least the above information.

DERIVATION

Information for the report is derived from:

- Observation and experience of the processes and techniques used
- Checkpoint Reports
- Observations of quality checks
- Performance against plans
- End Stage Reports
- Any exception situations.

PROCESSES INVOLVED

The Lessons Learned Report is updated at the end of each stage as part of the process 'Report Stage End' (SB5) and completed at the close of a project in the process 'Evaluate the Project' (CP3).

QUALITY CRITERIA

- Input to the report is being done, minimally, at the end of each stage
- Every management control has been examined
- A review of every specialist technique is included
- Statistics of the success of Quality Reviews and other types of quality check used are included
- The accuracy of all estimates and plans is included
- Details of the effort taken for each product are given
- The success of change control is reviewed.

Quality Method

Informal review at each stage end by the Project Manager and assurance team.

Formal Quality Review by this group before presentation.

Title: Project Mandate

Purpose

Project Mandate is a term to describe an initial request for a project, which may require further work to turn it into a Project Brief.

Composition

The actual composition of a Project Mandate will vary according to the type and size of project and also the environment in which the mandate is generated.

The following is a list of contents which would make up an 'ideal' mandate, and should be tailored to suit the specific project. An actual mandate may have much less information.

- Authority responsible
- The customer(s), user(s) and any other known interested parties
- Background
- Outline Business Case (reasons)
- Project objectives
- Scope
- Constraints
- Interfaces
- Quality expectations
- An estimate of the project size and duration (if known)
- A view of the risks faced by the project
- An indication of who should be the project Executive and Project Manager
- Reference to any associated projects or products.

FORM(AT)

May be in any form.

DERIVATION

A Project Mandate may come from anywhere, but it should come from a level of management which can authorise the cost and resource usage.

PROCESSES INVOLVED

It should be created before the project is triggered and input to the process 'Start Up the Project' (SU).

QUALITY CRITERIA

- Does the mandate describe what is required?
- Is the level of authority commensurate with the anticipated size, risk and cost of the project?
- Is there sufficient detail to allow the appointment of an appropriate Executive and Project Manager?
- Are all the known interested parties identified?

QUALITY METHOD

Informal review between Executive, Project Manager and the mandate author.

Title: Off-Specification

PURPOSE

An Off-Specification is a specific type of Project Issue. It is used to document any situation where a product or the project is failing, or is forecast to fail, to meet a target.

COMPOSITION

- Date
- Issue Log number
- Type (Off-Specification)
- Status

- Description of the problem
- Impact of the problem
- Priority assessment
- Decision
- Allocation details, if applicable
- Date allocated
- Date completed.

FORM(AT)

Same format as Project Issue.

DERIVATION

Can be raised by anyone associated with the project at any time.

PROCESSES INVOLVED

It would be gathered in as part of the process 'Capture Project Issues' (CS3). The Project Manager may also decide that a Project Issue is an Off-Specification during the process 'Examine Project Issues' (CS4).

QUALITY CRITERIA

- Logged in the Issue Log
- Accurate description of the problem.

QUALITY METHOD

Form completion checked by the person responsible for the Issue Log.

Checked on a regular basis by the person responsible for provider assurance.

Title: Project Brief

PURPOSE

To briefly explain the reasons for the project, the customer's expectations, and any limitations which apply.

COMPOSITION

The following is a suggested list of contents which should be tailored to the requirements and environment of each project.

- Project Definition, explaining what the project needs to achieve:
  - Background
  - Project objectives
  - Project scope
  - Outline project deliverables and/or desired outcomes
  - Any exclusions
  - Constraints
  - Interfaces
- Outline Business Case
  - Reason for the project
  - Description of how this project supports business strategy, plans or programmes
- Customer's Quality Expectations
- Acceptance Criteria
- Any known risks.

If earlier work has been done, the Project Brief may refer to document(s), such as Outline Project Plan.

FORM(AT)

Site project request standards containing at least the information shown above.

DERIVATION

- Project Mandate.
- If the project is part of a programme, the programme should provide the Project Brief.
- If no Project Mandate is provided, the Project Manager has to generate the Project Brief in discussions with the Customer and Users.
- Any significant change to the material contained in the Project Brief will thus need to be referred to corporate or programme management.

Processes Involved

It is developed from the Project Mandate supplied at the start of the project, produced by the process 'Start Up the Project' (SU), and accepted via 'Authorise Initiation' (DP1).

Quality Criteria

- Does it accurately reflect the Project Mandate?
- Does it form a firm basis on which to initiate a project (Initiate the Project (IP))?
- Does it indicate how the Customer will assess the acceptability of the finished product(s)?

Quality Method

Informal Quality Review between the Project Manager and the Project Board during the process 'Start Up the Project' (SU).

Title: Project Initiation Document

Purpose

- To define the project
- To form the basis for the ultimate assessment of the project's success and the project's management.

There are two primary uses of the document:

- to ensure that the project has a sound basis before asking the Project Board to make any major commitment to the project
- to act as a base document against which the Project Board and Project Manager can assess progress, evaluate change issues, and questions of the project's continuing viability.

Composition

The Project Initiation Document must answer these fundamental questions:

- What the project is aiming to achieve
- Why it is important to achieve it
- Who is going to be involved in managing the project and what are their responsibilities
- How and when it is all going to happen.

The following list should be seen as the information needed in order to make the initiation decisions.

- **Background**, explaining the context of the project, and steps taken to arrive at the current position of requiring a project.
- **Project Definition**, explaining what the project needs to achieve. Under this heading may be:
  - Project objectives
  - Project deliverables and/or desired outcomes
  - Project scope
  - Constraints
  - Exclusions
  - Defined method of approach (if applicable)
  - Interfaces.
- **Assumptions**
- **Initial Business Case**, explaining why the project is being undertaken
- **Project Organisation Structure**, defining the Project Management Team
- **Project Quality Plan** (See the separate Project Quality Plan Product Description)
- **Initial Project Plan**, explaining how and when the activities of the project will occur. (For details of the Project Plan content see the separate Product Description)
- **Project Controls**, stating how control is to be exercised within the project, and the reporting and monitoring mechanisms which will support this
- **Exception process**, the steps to be followed for any significant deviations
- **Initial Risk Log**, summarising the results of the risk analysis and risk management activities
- **Contingency Plans**, explaining how it is intended to deal with the consequences of any identified serious risks if they materialise
- **Project Filing Structure**, laying down how the various elements of information and deliverables produced by the project are to be filed and retrieved.

FORM(AT)

Site report standards.

DERIVATION

- Customer's or supplier's project management standards
- Customer's specified control requirements.

(Much of the information should come from the Project Mandate, enhanced in the Project Brief.)

PROCESSES INVOLVED

The Project Initiation Document is completed during the Initiation Stage. Versions of the Project Plan and Business Case may be updated and refined by each pass through the process 'Manage Stage Boundaries' (SB) and will finally be archived as part of the process 'Close the Project' (CP).

QUALITY CRITERIA

- Does the document correctly represent the project?
- Does it show a viable, achievable project which is in line with corporate strategy, or overall programme needs?
- Is the project organisation structure complete, with names and titles?
- Does it clearly show a control, reporting and direction regime which is implementable and appropriate to the scale, business risk and importance of the project?
- Has everyone named in the organisation structure received and accepted their job description?
- Does the project organisation structure need to say to whom the Project Board reports?
- Are the internal and external relationships and lines of authority clear?
- Do the controls cover the needs of the Project Board, Project Manager and any Team Managers?
- Do the controls satisfy any delegated assurance requirements?
- Is it clear who will administer each control?

QUALITY METHOD

Formal Quality Review between the Project Manager and those with assurance responsibilities.

Title: Post Implementation Review

PURPOSE

The purpose of the Post Implementation Review is to find out:

- Whether the expected benefits of the product have been realised
- If the product has caused any problems in use
- What enhancement opportunities have been revealed by use of the product.

Each expected benefit is assessed for the level of its achievement so far, any additional time needed for the benefit to materialise.

Unexpected side effects, beneficial or adverse, which use of the product may have brought, are documented with explanations of why these were not foreseen.

Recommendations are made to realise or improve benefits, or counter problems.

COMPOSITION

- Achievement of expected benefits
- Unexpected benefits
- Unexpected problems
- User reaction
- Follow-on work recommendations.

FORM(AT)

Site reporting standards.

DERIVATION

The expected benefits should have been defined in the Project Brief and expanded in the Project Initiation Document.

General comments should be obtained about how the Users feel about the product. The type of observation will depend on the type of product produced by the project, but examples might be its ease of use, performance, reliability, contribution it makes to their work, and suitability for the work environment.

PROCESSES INVOLVED

The Post Implementation Review is planned as part of the process 'Identify Follow-On Actions' (CP2), but the product itself is produced after the project has finished.

QUALITY CRITERIA

- Covers all benefits mentioned in the Project Brief and Business Case.
- Covers all changes approved during the project life cycle.
- Includes discussions with representatives of all those affected by the end product.
- Describes each achievement in a tangible, measurable form.
- Makes recommendations in cases where a benefit is not being fully provided, a problem has been identified, or a potential extra benefit could be obtained.
- Is conducted as soon as the benefits and problems can be measured.

QUALITY METHOD

Formal Quality Review against the Project Brief, Business Case and Issue Log.

Title: Project Quality Plan

PURPOSE

The purpose is to define how the supplier intends to deliver products which meet the customer's quality expectations and the agreed quality standards.

COMPOSITION

- Quality control and audit processes to be applied to project management
- Quality control and audit process requirements for specialist work

- Key product quality criteria
- Quality responsibilities
- Reference to any standards which need to be met
- Change management procedures
- Configuration management plan
- Any tools to be used to ensure quality.

FORM(AT)

The Project Quality Plan is part of the Project Initiation Document.

DERIVATION

- Customer's quality expectations (Project Mandate and/or Brief)
- Corporate or programme Quality Management System (QMS).

PROCESSES INVOLVED

It is produced as an output from the process 'Plan Project Quality' (IP1).

QUALITY CRITERIA

- Does the plan clearly define ways to confirm that the Customer's quality expectations will be met?
- Are the defined ways sufficient to achieve the required quality?
- Are responsibilities for quality defined up to a level which is independent of the project and Project Manager?
- Does the plan conform to corporate Quality Policy?

QUALITY METHOD

Review between the Project Manager and whoever is assuring the project on behalf of the customer.

Title: Product Checklist

PURPOSE

Lists the products to be produced within a plan, together with key status dates. Updated at agreed reporting intervals by the Project Manager and used by the Project Board to monitor progress.

COMPOSITION

- Plan identification
- Product names (and identifiers where appropriate)
- Planned and actual dates for:
  - Draft product ready
  - Quality check
  - Approval

FORM(AT)

Standard department form with the headings defined under 'Composition'.

DERIVATION

Extracted from the Stage Plan.

PROCESSES INVOLVED

Produced as an output from process 'Complete the Plan' (PL7).

QUALITY CRITERIA

Do the details and dates match those in the plan?

QUALITY METHOD

Informal review against the plan.

Title: Project Plan

PURPOSE

A mandatory plan which shows at a high level how and when a project's objectives are to be achieved. It contains the major products of the project, the activities and resources required.

It provides the Business Case with planned project costs, and identifies the management stages and other major control points.

It is used by the Project Board as a baseline against which to monitor project progress and cost stage by stage.

It forms part of the Project Initiation Document.

COMPOSITION

- Plan description, giving a brief description of what the plan covers
- Project pre-requisites, containing any fundamental aspects which must be in place at the start of the project, and which must remain in place for the project to succeed
- External dependencies
- Planning assumptions
- Project Plan, covering:
  - Project level Gantt or bar chart with identified management stages
  - Project level Product Breakdown Structure
  - Project level Product Flow Diagrams
  - Project level Product Descriptions
  - Project level activity network.
  - Project financial budget
  - Project level table of resource requirements
  - Requested/assigned specific resources.

FORM(AT)

Gantt or Bar Chart plus text.

DERIVATION

Project Brief.

PROCESSES INVOLVED

Refined from the outline Project Plan in the Project Brief during the process 'Plan the Project' (IP2). Modified during the process 'Update the Project Plan' (SB2).

QUALITY CRITERIA

- Is the plan achievable?
- Does it support the rest of the Project Initiation Document?

QUALITY METHOD

Formal Quality Review with Project Manager and those with assurance responsibilities.

Title: Quality Log

PURPOSE

- To issue a unique reference for each quality check or test planned.
- To act as a pointer to the quality check and test documentation for a product.
- To act as a summary of the number and type of quality checks and tests held.

The log summarises all the quality checks and tests which are planned/ have taken place, and provides information for the End Stage and End Project Reports, as well as the Lessons Learned Report.

COMPOSITION

For each entry in the log:

- Quality check reference number
- Product checked or tested
- Planned date of the check
- Actual date of the check
- Result of the check
- Number of action items found
- Target sign-off date
- Actual Sign-off date.

FORM(AT)

Standard departmental form with the headings shown in 'Composition'.

DERIVATION

The first entries are made when a quality check or test is entered on a Stage Plan. The remaining information comes from the actual performance of the check. The sign-off date is when all corrective action items have been signed off.

PROCESSES INVOLVED

The blank Quality Log is created during the process 'Set Up Project Files' (IP5).

QUALITY CRITERIA

- Is there a procedure in place which will ensure that every quality check is entered on the log?
- Has responsibility for the log been allocated?

QUALITY METHOD

Regular checking should be done by those with assurance responsibilities for the customer and provider. There may also be an inspection by an independent quality assurance function.

Title: Request For Change

PURPOSE

To request a modification to a product or an acceptance criterion as currently specified.

COMPOSITION

- Date
- Issue Log number
- Class
- Status
- Description of the proposed change
- Impact of the change
- Priority assessment
- Decision
- Allocation details, if applicable
- Date allocated
- Date completed.

FORM(AT)

The same form as the Project Issue.

DERIVATION

Anyone connected with the project.

PROCESSES INVOLVED

A Request For Change can be submitted as such and gathered in by the process 'Capture Project Issues' (CS3), or a Project Issue can be redefined as a Request For Change by the Project Manager as part of the process 'Examine Project Issues' (CS4).

QUALITY CRITERIA

- Source of the request clearly identified
- Logged in the Issue Log
- Accurate description of the requested change
- Supported by any necessary evidence
- Benefit of making the change clearly expressed and, where possible, in measurable terms.

QUALITY METHOD

Initial review by those with assurance responsibilities, if any of these are delegated by the Project Board.

Confirmation of the type by the Project Manager.

Title: Risk Log

PURPOSE

The purpose of the Risk Log is to:

- allocate a unique number to each risk
- record the type of risk
- be a summary of the risks, their analysis and status.

COMPOSITION

- Risk number
- Risk type (business, project, stage)
- Author
- Date risk identified
- Date of last risk status update
- Risk description

- Likelihood
- Severity
- Countermeasure(s)
- Status
- Responsible.

FORM(AT)

Standard department form with the headings shown in 'Composition'.

DERIVATION

Business risks may have been identified in the Project Brief and should be sought during Project Initiation. There should be a check for any new risks every time the Risk Log is reviewed or a new plan made, minimally at each End Stage Assessment.

The Project Board has the responsibility to constantly check external events for business risks.

PROCESSES INVOLVED

The Risk Log is created during the process 'Prepare the Project Brief' (SU4).

Project risks are sought during Project Initiation when the Project Plan is being created. Some risks may have been identified in work which led up to the Project Mandate. All risks to the success of the project should be re-assessed every time the Risk Log is reviewed, minimally at each End Stage Assessment.

Risks to a Stage Plan should be examined as part of the production of that plan. They should also be reviewed each time a plan is updated.

QUALITY CRITERIA

- Does the status indicate whether action has been/is being taken or is in a contingency plan?
- Are the risks uniquely identified, including to which product they refer?
- Is access to the Risk Log controlled?
- Is the Risk Log kept in a safe place?
- Are activities to review the Risk Log in the stage plans?

- Has responsibility for monitoring the risk been identified and documented?

QUALITY METHOD

Regular review by the person who has business assurance responsibility.

Title: Stage Plan

PURPOSE

- Identifies the products which the stage must produce
- Provides a statement of how and when a stage's objectives are to be achieved
- Identifies the stage's control and reporting points and frequencies
- Provides a baseline against which stage progress will be measured
- Records the stage tolerances
- Specifies the quality controls for the stage and the resources needed for them.

COMPOSITION

- Plan Description
- Stage Quality Plan
- Plan Prerequisites
- External Dependencies
- Tolerances (time and budget)
- How will the plan be monitored and controlled?
- Reporting
- Planning Assumptions
- Graphical Plan, showing identified resources, activities, start and end dates (usually a Gantt or Bar Chart)
- Financial budget
- Table of resource requirements
- Risk assessment
- Product Descriptions for the major products.

FORM(AT)

Graphical plan plus text.

DERIVATION

- Project Plan
- Based on resource availability.

PROCESSES INVOLVED

Refined from the Project Plan during the process 'Plan a Stage' (SB1).

Updated during 'Assess Progress' (CS2). May be modified during 'Report Stage End' (SB5) and 'Take Corrective Action' (CS7).

QUALITY CRITERIA

- Is the plan achievable?
- Do any Team Managers involved in its operation believe that their portion is achievable?
- Does it support the Project Plan?
- Does it take into account any constraints of time, resources and budget?
- Has the plan been taken down to the level of detail necessary to ensure that any deviations will be recognised in time to react appropriately? (e.g. within the stage tolerances, and within the activity 'floats'.)
- Has it been developed according to the planning standard?
- Does the Stage Plan contain activities and resource effort to review the Issue Log?

QUALITY METHOD

Review by the Project Manager and those with assurance responsibilities.

Title: Work Package

PURPOSE

A set of instructions to produce one or more required products given by the Project Manager to a Team Manager or team member.

COMPOSITION

Although the content may vary greatly according to the relationship between the Project Manager and the recipient of the Work Package, it should cover:

- A summary of the work to be done
- Product Description(s) of the products to be produced
- Standards to be used
- Product interfaces
- Working interfaces and liaisons
- Quality checking standards, personnel to be involved.

FORM(AT)

This product will vary in content and in degree of formality, depending on circumstances. Where the work is being conducted by a single team working directly for the Project Manager, the Work Package may be a verbal instruction, although there are good reasons for putting it in writing, such as avoidance of misunderstanding and providing a link to performance assessment.

Where the work is being carried out by a supplier under a contract and the Project Manager is part of the customer organisation, the Work Package should be a formal, written document.

DERIVATION

There could be many Work Packages authorised during each stage. A Work Package is created by the Project Manager from the Stage Plan.

PROCESSES INVOLVED

The process 'Authorise Work Package' (CS1) covers the issue of Work Packages. After the initial start of a stage subsequent Work Packages will be triggered after the process 'Review Stage Status' (CS5). Changes to the Stage Plan brought about when performing the process 'Take Corrective Action' (CS7) may also trigger the authorisation of new Work Packages.

Quality Criteria

- Is the required Work Package clearly defined and understood by the assigned resource?
- Is there a Product Description for the required product(s) with clearly identified and acceptable quality criteria?
- Does the Product Description match up with the other Work Package documentation?
- Are standards for the work agreed?
- Are the defined standards in line with those applied to similar products?
- Have all necessary interfaces been defined?
- Do the reporting arrangements include the provision for exception reporting?

Quality Method

Agreement between the Project Manager and recipient.

Title: Work Package Authorisation

Purpose

To formally pass responsibility for work or delivery to a Team Manager or team member.

A Work Package Authorisation forms a 'contract' between the Project Manager and the Team Manager or team member who receives it.

Composition

The content may vary greatly according to the relationship between the Project Manager and the recipient of the Work Package Authorisation, but should cover:

- Date
- Team or person authorised
- Work Package reference

- Stage Plan extract
- Joint agreement on effort, cost, start and end dates
- Work approval and return arrangements
- Reporting requirements.

FORM(AT)

This product will vary in form and content, and indeed in degree of formality, depending on project circumstances. Where the work is being conducted by a team working directly under the Project Manager, the Work Package Authorisation may be a verbal instruction. Where the work is being carried out by a supplier under a contract, there is a need for a formal, written authorisation.

DERIVATION

A Work Package Authorisation is created by the Project Manager from the Stage Plan. There will be many Work Packages authorised during each stage.

PROCESSES INVOLVED

This is covered by the process 'Authorise Work Package' (CS1). After the initial start of a stage subsequent Work Package Authorisations will be triggered after 'Review Stage Status' (CS5). Changes to the Stage Plan brought about when 'Take Corrective Action' (CS7) may also trigger new Work Package Authorisations.

QUALITY CRITERIA

- Is the required Work Package clearly defined and understood by the assigned resource?
- Is there agreement between the Project Manager and the recipient on exactly what is to be done?
- Is there agreement on the constraints, including effort, cost and targets?
- Is there a Product Description with clearly identified and acceptable quality criteria?
- Does the Product Description match up with the other Work Package documentation?

- Are standards for the work agreed?
- Are the defined standards in line with those applied to similar products?
- Are the dates and effort in line with those shown in the Stage Plan?
- Have all necessary interfaces been defined?
- Do the reporting arrangements include the provision for exception reporting?

QUALITY METHOD

Agreement between the Project Manager and the recipient.

Index